"I'll Try" Is Not
Good Enough . . .

"I'll Try" Is Not Good Enough . . .

What It Takes to Make Change Happen in the Workplace!

Philip B. Nelson
Kirk W. Nelson
Michael J. Paxton

authorHOUSE®

AuthorHouse™
1663 Liberty Drive
Bloomington, IN 47403
www.authorhouse.com
Phone: 1-800-839-8640

© 2010, 2012 by Philip B. Nelson Kirk W. Nelson Michael J. Paxton. All rights reserved.

No part of this book may be reproduced, stored in a retrieval system, or transmitted by any means without the written permission of the author.

First published by AuthorHouse   01/18/2012

ISBN: 978-1-4685-0928-1 (sc)
ISBN: 978-1-4685-0927-4 (ebk)

Library of Congress Control Number: 2011961756

Printed in the United States of America

Any people depicted in stock imagery provided by Thinkstock are models, and such images are being used for illustrative purposes only.
Certain stock imagery © Thinkstock.

Because of the dynamic nature of the Internet, any web addresses or links contained in this book may have changed since publication and may no longer be valid. The views expressed in this work are solely those of the author and do not necessarily reflect the views of the publisher, and the publisher hereby disclaims any responsibility for them.

This book is dedicated to the memory of Philip B. Nelson, PhD.

His long and illustrious career started in the 1970's when he established his independent management consultant practice. Over the years, he worked with a variety of corporations from family-owned businesses to Fortune 500 companies.

His background as a clinical psychologist made him adept in his understanding of how the individual could grow and change according to the position in which he or she was placed within an organization. His expertise included executive coaching and development, organizational design and structure, program implementation, cultural assessment and change, executive selection, succession planning, family business transition, and board formation and development.

He has published several books that have encompassed topics varying from stress analysis to the secrets of leadership that have been widely embraced by both the medical community and the business world. Over the years, he saw that change and the ability to change is critical, which is why he wanted to write this final publication and share his years of knowledge and experience. He will be greatly missed by all of his loyal clients, as well as by his beloved family, to whom he dedicated his life and ideas.

CONTENTS

Acknowledgments ix
Preface xi
Introduction xiii

Part One Why Change Is Difficult 1

Chapter One   Understanding Capacity 3
Chapter Two   Awareness and Feedback Deficiencies 7
Chapter Three   External Motivation 22
Chapter Four   Internal Motivation 30
Chapter Five   Lack of Education and Training.............. 38

Part Two Facilitating Change 45

Chapter Six   Dealing With Capacity Issues 47
Chapter Seven   Correcting Deficiencies in Awareness:
                         Feedback Deficiencies............................ 53
Chapter Eight   Creating External Motivation 64
Chapter Nine   Altering Internal Motivation................... 70
Chapter Ten   Creating a Climate for Development 83

Conclusion 89
Appendix.. 92
    Advice on Utilizing Consultants 93
    Bibliography.. 96
    About the Authors.. 98

ACKNOWLEDGMENTS

The authors wish to thank Jan vanderVoort, Ken Royal, Mike Marovich, and Paul Carter for their contributions in helping us to move the content of this book from theoretical to practical. Without their assistance, it would have been more difficult to achieve our goal—to create a workbook that is easily understandable and with content that can be readily applied by managers on a day-to-day basis.

PREFACE

This is a workbook for managers to help them effectively deal with their employees and with the process of change. Today's business world is dynamic and ever evolving; managers must learn to adapt for their growth and that of the organization. Change is the new constant.

And yet change is generally the most difficult factor for managers to confront effectively in the workplace. The paradox is that the measure of success in any organization is the quality and effectiveness of its human resources. It is the people at every level of a company, with their collective skill set, competencies, and commitment, that advance the mission and profitability of an organization.

Hiring the right people for the right positions from the beginning is crucial to success. In *Good to Great*, author Jim Collins emphasizes that the executives who ignited the transformation from good to great first "got the right people on the bus and the wrong people off the bus and the right people in the right seats." He said, in essence, that if we can make this happen, we will figure out how to take the company someplace great.

Managers must start with disciplined selection and hiring practices, get people in the right positions, and then begin their development. Especially with new hires, managers must identify the gaps and quickly begin to deal with them before they get set in patterns that are not conducive to their success in the organization. As a result of companies' leadership and unique histories, they generally have special cultures that develop over time. For newcomers, the "fit" can prove to be a big challenge. A person's fit must first be recognized so that it can then be worked on from the beginning. This can assure a much smoother transition for the individual into the company; however, the more experienced a new person is, the more difficult the fit may be.

Apart from what is genetically inherited, personalities and behavioral patterns start to develop at an early stage of an individual's life. They are not easy to change. Given that truism, it is imperative that managers find ways to modify the organizational culture in order to encourage the development and adaptation of their employees' performance to the demands of their business and the marketplace.

It takes a conscientious effort on the part of management (who may already feel overextended) to devote the necessary time to meaningfully educate, coach, and mentor those who work for them. It is important that people remind themselves to set aside this time in their schedules. One's role as a teacher and developer of people is critical for the future of the company. *When the manager creates a "can-do" commitment instead of an "I'll-try" attitude, it can be the difference between success and mediocrity.*

Our goal in writing this workbook is to provide practical information that any manager can understand and apply on a daily basis.

INTRODUCTION

As managers, consultants, board members, and employees, the authors—the late Philip B. Nelson, PhD; Kirk Nelson, MFA; and Mike Paxton—have served in a variety of businesses, nonprofit endeavors, and creative/artistic positions. We have experience in companies like Fox Broadcasting Company, Foster Farms, Inc., J. P. Morgan, Mattel, Inc., National Semiconductor, Hewlett-Packard, Clorox, General Electric, Pfizer Pharmaceuticals, American Broadcasting Company, the Urban Land Institute, Pillsbury, Häagen-Dazs, Sunbeam, and O-Cedar Holdings, Inc. What we've learned will help you work with your staff more effectively and also help you to implement needed change.

To help you deal with change, this workbook will show you major principles of human behavior, teach you how to deal with that behavior, and help you make changes to manage that behavior in the workplace. We've created ten principles that focus on change. Principles 1-5 focus on why change is difficult, and principles 6-10 focus on the methods of achieving it.

Principle 1: Some people may lack the innate capacity that is necessary to perform in their jobs most effectively.

Principle 2: Individuals cannot change behavior that limits their performance if they are unaware of this behavior and its consequences.

Principle 3: Individuals tend not to change their behavior unless they perceive the resulting consequences of such change to be more favorable than the consequences of their current behavior.

Principle 4: Individuals' self-perception, not reality, defines who they are and how they behave. Self-perception is resistant to change and can prevent individuals from altering their behavior.

Principle 5: Never assume that an individual has the necessary competence and training to do the job. You must probe and test for evidence and solicit feedback that the training exists.

Principle 6: New behavior, called "overlays," can be learned by individuals without altering their genetic capacity or "hardwiring." These overlays allow individuals to behave or act in a different but more effective manner.

Principle 7: Individuals, in order to create awareness, need consistent, specific verbal and written feedback. This is necessary in order to overcome interpersonal, systems, and internal "screens" (self-perception). This feedback must come from managers and others with whom the individuals work.

Principle 8: Individuals must have greater incentive to change their behaviors than to leave their behaviors unchanged.

"I'll Try" Is Not Good Enough ...

Principle 9: Meaningful and lasting change may require that individuals alter the ways in which they perceive themselves. It requires patience and discipline in order to achieve this. Self-perception can be altered, but not without real effort. It requires a well-thought-out plan, strong rewards, and discipline.

Principle 10: A developmental climate and proper training must occur for individuals to acquire the competence and skill sets to perform successfully in their positions.

These principles will help you manage the concept of change—and get it across to your staff—more effectively. Each chapter has room for notes so that you can jot down ideas, examples, and concepts regarding change that will apply to your own life and those of your staff.

If people could change their competencies and characteristics at will, personal development would be a relatively simple matter. However, there are many reasons why people consciously or unconsciously tend to resist change.

The purpose of this book is to make you aware of techniques for overcoming resistance to change and to help you meaningfully influence the change processes of others. Knowledge of these techniques will allow you to formulate and execute truly effective personal planning and development.

An individual's behavior is a function of his or her innate capacity, level of awareness, motivation, and competence to execute his or her work responsibilities.

> *Behavior*
> =
> [Capacity] x [Awareness] x [Motivation] x [Execution]

Behavior is profoundly influenced by each of these factors. Positively impacting an individual is essentially a matter of altering one or more of these factors that impede behavior change. This is reflected in the following diagram.

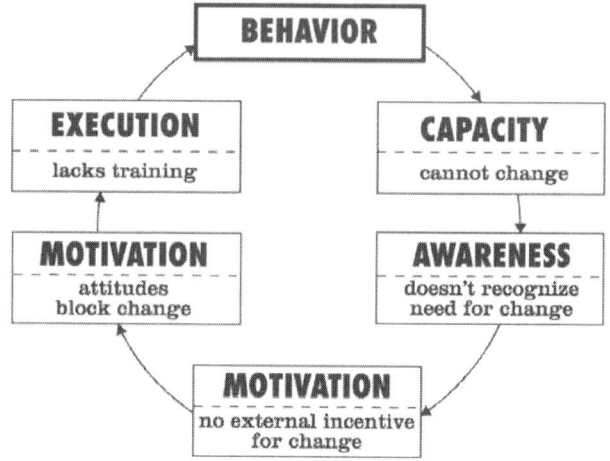

Figure 1. The Cycle of Behavior Change

Once you understand the basic concepts of capacity, awareness, motivation, and education/training, you'll understand why change is difficult for people. Then you can help to facilitate change by dealing with capacity issues, awareness deficiencies, and external and internal motivations. Then you can create a climate for lasting change.

"I'll Try" Is Not Good Enough . . .

When "I'll try" isn't a good enough response, use these concepts to help your company grow and change.

In the next chapter, "Understanding Capacity," we'll review Principle 1 and see how it affects an individual's work style.

PART ONE
WHY CHANGE IS DIFFICULT

CHAPTER ONE

UNDERSTANDING CAPACITY

Principle 1: *Some people may lack the innate capacity that is necessary to perform in their jobs most effectively.*

LIMITED CAPACITY—After decades of experience in various professional fields, we've found that individuals may be missing the necessary capacity to achieve the desired change.

An individual is "hardwired" in a variety of ways by his or her genetic background. As a consequence, some of the behavior—which is genetically ingrained—is hard, if not impossible, to change. Ability and capacity are often confused. Ability can be defined as one's competence in performing a specific learned task, whereas capacity refers to the physical capability to perform and the mental acuity to follow through.

The individual may have the ability to perform a given task that he or she has learned, but it must follow in his or her innate capacity to do so.

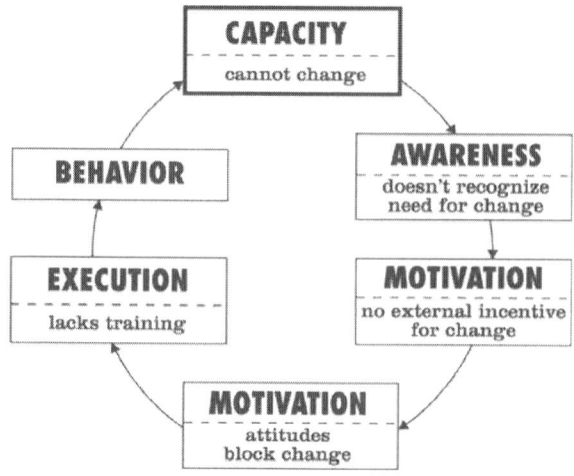

The following are some areas where limited capacity may play a more important role:

- the capacity to analyze and solve complex problems
- sensitivity and empathy with regard to people
- the capacity to grasp more abstract, conceptual issues
- physical skills and abilities
- creativity and the ability to "think out of the box"
- a sense of time and its role in the workplace
- right brain (free-form/out-of-the-box thinking)/left brain (more sequential thinking)
- introversion/extroversion

According to research by the late Psychologist Richard J. Herrnstein and Charles Murray, it has been shown that these areas of capacity tend to vary according to a bell-shaped curve with the majority of people falling in the middle. This is depicted in the graph below.

"I'll Try" Is Not Good Enough . . .

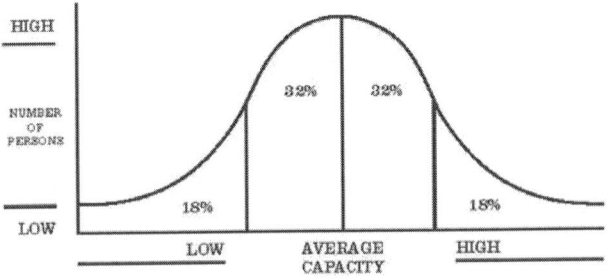

As a manager, you should attempt to determine whether or not an individual has the innate capacity to succeed in the position by using an IQ test. Since, for the most part, capacity does not change, accurate assessments in this area may be critical when an individual is hired for a position or transferred to a new position. The higher the position, the greater the innate capacity an individual may need for success in the position. As you well know, many individuals from CEO down have failed, because they were promoted beyond the level of their capacity. If an individual truly lacks the capacity, one may not want to put out the effort to try to achieve change.

Deficiencies that appear to reflect lack of capacity, however, can and do frequently stem from other impediments to behavior change. It may be necessary to probe all of the other impediments to change before reaching a conclusion. For example, individuals may not believe that they have the capacity to succeed in a given area—when actually they do—and it is their limiting self-perception that is holding them back.

Summary

A person's capacity for learning and change will directly affect his or her performance on the job. Once you've determined capacity, it's time to explore a person's awareness of his or her behavior. We'll review that topic in the next chapter, "Awareness and Feedback Deficiencies."

Notes

CHAPTER TWO

AWARENESS AND FEEDBACK DEFICIENCIES

Principle 2: *Individuals cannot change behavior that limits their performance if they are unaware of this behavior and its consequences.*

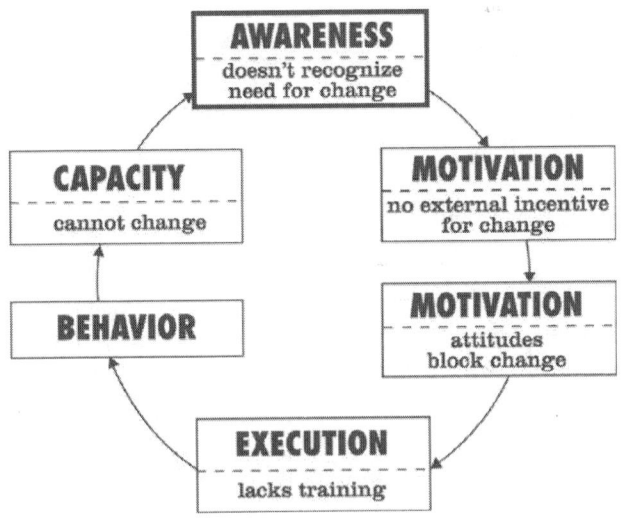

Limited awareness means that an individual doesn't recognize the need for change. An individual may have the capacity to change but may not be aware that change is necessary. A primary reason why individuals do not change is that they lack this personal awareness along with the specific information indicating why and/or what they need to change.

A good example of this is Mary L.

> Mary was an engaging and intelligent young software salesperson who had everything going for her. She was organized, personable, knowledgeable, and generally competent. Yet, she was underachieving. She couldn't generate commissions. She wasn't opening accounts. As her manager, the first day I called her, I knew part of the reason for her failure. She lacked assertiveness and seemed anxious on the phone. Her prospective clients might well have concluded that she lacked confidence and, in turn, decided not to do business with her. When questioned on this issue, it became totally apparent that Mary was unaware of her behavior and the impact it was having.

Accurate, ongoing feedback has long been identified as a necessary factor in producing behavior change. In Mary's case, lack of feedback was her main problem. Once she realized how she was being perceived by her prospective clients, it allowed her to formulate a plan to change her behavior and execute it. It worked wonders!

Humans need feedback to recognize how they are currently functioning and how they might function more effectively. Even without deficiencies, self-induced or otherwise, we are biologically handicapped. In order to not go into overload, our sensors allow us to perceive only a small portion of our total environment. For example, we can see only a small percentage of the spectrum of light and hear only a small percentage of the range of sound. Our senses of smell, touch, and taste are primitive, to say the least. This is true in all of our functioning senses and can be revealed in both our personal and business lives.

As if this were not enough, individuals can habitually create and maintain feedback deficiencies in those areas that they work in. Feedback deficiencies are created by a lack of clear, consistent, and frequent feedback. There are three types of feedback deficiencies:

- those created by a lack of or unclear "feedback systems" in which the individual must work
- those created by the individuals themselves as a result of their limiting self-perceptions
- those created by personal and systems deficiencies

We'll discuss these deficiencies further.

Interpersonal Feedback Deficiencies

A useful reference for our discussion of interpersonal feedback deficiencies is a model known as the Johari Window. This model defines the effects that occur in situations ranging from perfect feedback conditions to totally imperfect feedback conditions.

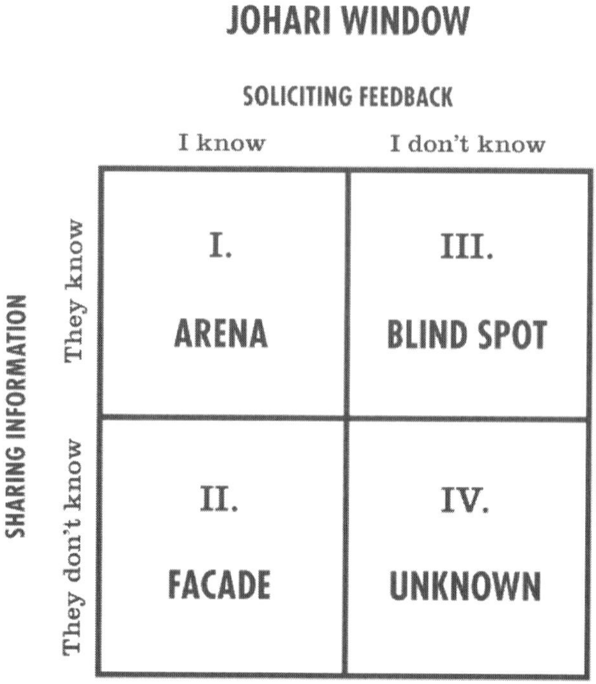

JOHARI WINDOW

SOLICITING FEEDBACK

	I know	I don't know
They know	I. ARENA	III. BLIND SPOT
They don't know	II. FACADE	IV. UNKNOWN

SHARING INFORMATION

Figure 2. The Johari Window

If everyone functioned as depicted in Quadrant I of the model, interpersonal feedback deficiencies would be minimal. Your goal as a manager must be to behave in ways that create the largest "arena" possible and to encourage your subordinates to do the same. Sharing information tends to perpetuate the process of receiving information.

"I'll Try" Is Not Good Enough...

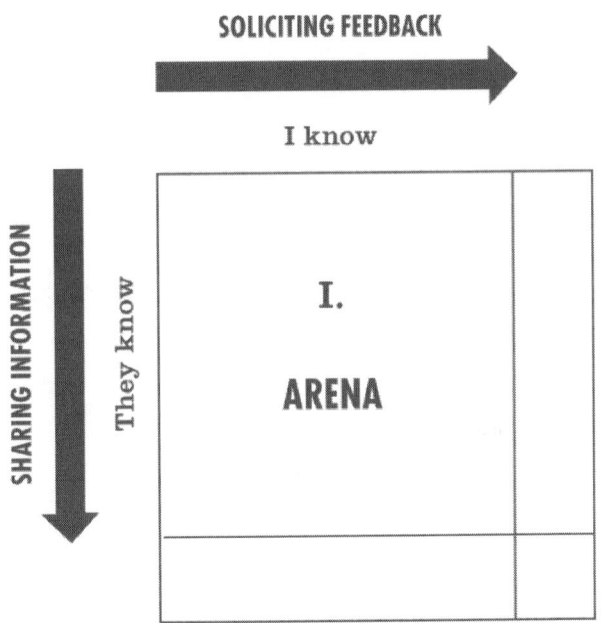

An "arena" describes a state in which you have an open loop of feedback coming to you from others and in which you are actively giving feedback to others and sharing with others feedback about yourself. In order to maintain this state, you must actively pursue it on a consistent and regular basis. Remember, the process of sharing information perpetuates the process of receiving information.

A facade is depicted by people who behave predominately in the Quadrant II arena. They actively seek information from others in order to be able to maintain control over a variety of situations (soliciting feedback). Conversely, they give little information and are private individuals about whom little is known. Maintenance of a facade is usually a defensive maneuver that some people feel is necessary in order to preserve relationships or image. In fact, it can build a lack of trust among others and can create the perception of phoniness.

A good example of a facade is Fred T.

> Fred was a twenty-nine-year-old West Coast restaurant manager who was well groomed, articulate, and very persuasive. He was an individual who always seemed to have the answers. He showed few signs of weakness, yet he was quick to point out weaknesses in others. Although he was effective in getting performance from his people, most subordinates indicated that they didn't know him very well. On a management effectiveness survey, Fred rated his group as high on the trust factor. His subordinates, however, rated it as very low. Fred was surprised at the outcome. He didn't realize that his facade was building barriers between himself and his employees and creating a rather low level of trust.

People who behave as described in Quadrant III are unaware of their impact on the workplace environment or on other people. Not only do they not solicit feedback, they may actively discourage it. A blind spot is an area in people's perceptions where they have trouble seeing themselves as others see them.

The following example of John F. illustrates the "blind spot" phenomenon.

> John F., a forty-two-year-old production service manager in a large eastern manufacturing corporation, was a very intelligent ex-college track star. He started working for

"I'll Try" Is Not Good Enough . . .

the corporation immediately following graduation. An extremely amiable person, he worked his way up to his current position through persistence and a great deal of effort. Recently, John's manager, the vice president of operations, decided that he had too broad a span of control and wanted to consolidate several functions, including production service, under one manager. After reviewing his inside management, including John, a decision was made to fill the position from the outside. John was devastated by the decision and felt that he had performed well over the years and earned the opportunity. When he confronted his boss with his disappointment, his boss replied, "We went to the outside, John, because I felt we needed a stronger, more experienced person for the position. This is not criticism of your competence; I think you are doing a fine job."

John asked his peers for feedback. He was told that he did not display a high enough sense of urgency and was not perceived as tough minded enough, something his boss had never relayed to him. The perception he held of himself and that his boss and peers held of him was a total blind spot. John was left with a disappointing perspective as to why the decision was made and why feedback wasn't provided. He was left with a diminished self-image and a decreased level of motivation.

It is obvious that John's management failed him miserably. Unfortunately, however, people with blind spots are often allowed to suffer the consequences, because it takes great effort for others to influence their behavior. In the end, many managers are reluctant to give honest feedback out of fear of hurting feelings and the conflict it may create. This management systems breakdown is a gross disservice to the individual.

The "unknown" quadrant is referred to as the "turtle" position, because it usually applies to security-minded individuals who rarely try anything new. Neither they nor those around them have access to any information about them. They have difficulty seeing themselves realistically and tend not to solicit feedback from others. Quadrant IV generally describes a severely troublesome and limiting condition.

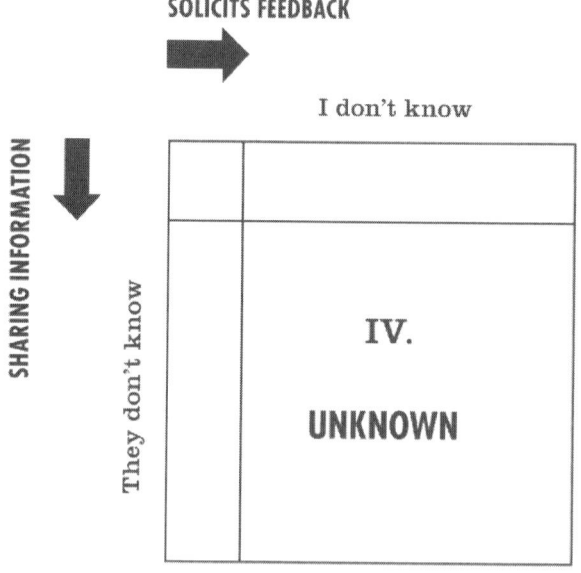

The following example illustrates the "unknown" or the "turtle" position.

> Jean S. was an accounting manager in a moderately large western semiconductor manufacturing company. She

was the type of individual who kept to herself most of the time and limited her interactions with others to those matters with which she had to deal. She stuck with tried-and-true methods and could be counted on to oppose change or new procedures. She solicited little input from others. She was attentive to the task aspects of her job and put up with people only because she had to. People knew little about her. Jean had a very low level of self-insight, was security oriented, and generally operated in a defensive, rigid mode.

In addition to personal feedback deficiencies, systems deficiencies can also have a strong effect on performance.

Systems Feedback Deficiency

Individuals experience a "systems feedback" deficiency when a process or system in an area of their work fails to provide them with sufficient information to adequately manage it.

We discovered an interesting systems feedback deficiency while developing a sales training program for stockbrokers. During our study of their training needs, it became clear that broker productivity was a function of the amount of time spent in contact with clients in the actual process of selling products or services ("selling time"). Although a lot of other facets of the brokers' time were looked at, for simplicity's sake, it was decided to lump all other activities into a category called "non-selling time." This included servicing existing accounts, doing research, analyzing stocks, and planning sales calls.

The brokers were asked to show as accurately as possible how their time was divided between these two types of activities. They estimated, on average, that they spent a minimum of two hours of selling time each day. For someone who makes his or her living by selling, this is not an impressive figure. When the brokers' selling and non-selling time was actually tracked, it was discovered that, on average, brokers spent only thirty minutes per day selling. Clearly, their beliefs and reality differed widely.

A program was established to increase the brokers' selling time to two hours per day. As a result, bottom-line performance increased 104 percent. When the feedback deficiency was corrected and the brokers had access to accurate information about their time allocations, they were able to execute the necessary behavior change to increase their productivity. Within the week, they implemented a system of charting time spent and the way it was spent.

This study was carried further, and such factors as the professional makeup of the clientele and success rates with differing age groups were analyzed. Other significant feedback deficiencies were discovered.

Systems feedback deficiencies can exist in a multitude of task-related areas. In each case, the result is the same. People can be unaware of their true performance levels.

A few years ago, an air freight forwarder set out to identify and correct systems feedback deficiencies within the organization. Feedback deficiencies were discovered everywhere in the organization—from line workers to the company telephone operators.

Deficiencies identified within the organization were as follows:

- inappropriate use of freight forwarding containers
- inefficient routing
- not responding to the number of call-in phone orders within a specific and respective time frame—four rings in this case

A program of tracking different performance areas and providing ongoing feedback was implemented. Correcting these feedback deficiencies resulted in substantial performance improvement and a significant increase in profit to the company.

Other intrapersonal deficiencies can also impact performance.

Intrapersonal Feedback Deficiencies

The third type of feedback deficiency develops within an individual—what we call "intrapersonal feedback" deficiencies. To understand how this occurs, some basic concepts must be examined.

Humans have a built-in screening mechanism that only allows information they perceive as being of value or threat to reach a conscious level and to be mentally absorbed. This important function allows them to automatically disregard a vast amount of irrelevant information and to focus on what is essential to their survival and well-being. Dr. Maxwell Maltz, in his book *Psycho-Cybernetics*, pointed out both the critical necessity and problems caused by this screening mechanism. If we couldn't filter all of the data around us, it could be overwhelming and impede our ability to function effectively. On the other hand, what constitutes value or threat is a complex issue. Other than basic survival input, it tends to vary from individual to individual based upon personal learning history. Because of this, in many ways, people tend to live in their own worlds and may filter out information that is critical to their success.

A good example of this is Jan L.

> Jan managed a building materials store and was very successful at it. Since the store was relatively small, she could easily stay on top of everything. Because of her success, she was promoted to manage one of the larger stores. She began to experience serious frustration during her first month. She couldn't stay on top of everything herself and needed to rely on others for support. She kept falling further behind, and her store's performance declined. She found herself constantly pointing out supply issues, merchandising issues, and other such issues to her staff. She was very frustrated and felt that these were things that they should have seen and corrected but did not.

What do you think the problem was here? Since Jan tended to see all of the issues personally, her staff didn't need to see the issues. The issues weren't important or of value to them, so they got screened out. This occurred unconsciously on their part. They knew that she would catch everything and that they didn't have to. As a consequence, they actually didn't see them.

Her solution to the problem was to change her behavior from telling to asking. When an issue became visible to her,

"I'll Try" Is Not Good Enough . . .

instead of pointing out the problem, she went to a given area of the store and asked her staff what the problem was. If they didn't have an answer, she would say, "Keep looking until you discover it." By doing this and not pointing out the issues herself, she was able to transfer ownership from herself to those that worked for her. Ownership and its consequences created value, allowing the information to get through their screens. Over time, the members of her staff began to see and solve the problems themselves. The performance of the store improved, and Jan's job got much easier.

You can see this mechanism at work in everyday life. It's the mechanism that allows people to deal effectively with the noise and bustle of a jammed airport—by screening out most of the assault on their senses—yet still allowing them to immediately perceive when their names are called over the loudspeaker. It's this mechanism that awakens a mother in profoundly deep sleep to full consciousness at her baby's quiet whimper.

Again, this screening mechanism maintains one's perception of the world by only allowing information that is of value or threat to get through. Growing from childhood into adulthood, individuals develop sets of beliefs about who they are, what they can and cannot do, and how they should behave in their personal and professional lives. In other words, it defines their place in the world. Throughout their daily lives, they have experiences that support and confirm these beliefs, reinforcing and strengthening them.

An individual's screens work to filter out information that is inconsistent with his or her beliefs, a process that can create substantial blind spots. It tends to perpetuate one's existing belief system, much of which may be faulty or inaccurate. It, in fact, may perpetuate a view of the world that may be quite different from reality. Behaving differently from one's self-perception creates dissonance, anxiety, and a feeling of dissociation, this, in turn, creates motivation to return to behaving like one's self. As a result, it is a self-perpetuating system.

This system of screening impacts people's lives by viewing events in a way that is consistent with their belief systems. For example, individuals may perceive themselves as poor public speakers—disorganized, anxious, and ineffective in front of large groups. When speaking to a large group, whether or not the actual performance is poor, individuals' perceptions tend to be consistent with their belief systems. In scanning the audience, individuals' attentions are drawn to those people who are showing disinterest or disapproval, and they tend to overlook those who are reacting positively. Regardless of actual competence, the belief systems cause those events that are inconsistent to be filtered out and self-perceptions to be maintained.

You need to be aware of the fact that much of the information or feedback you give an employee, in an attempt to modify his or her behavior, may be screened out by the individual's filtering mechanism. In many ways, it resembles an unconscious form of denial.

Summary
Awareness deficiencies—be they interpersonal, systems, or intrapersonal—contribute greatly to an individual's inability to change. Interpersonal feedback deficiencies are focused on an individual's interaction with others. Systems feedback

deficiencies are centered on an organization's processes and procedures. Intrapersonal feedback deficiencies deal with an individual's internal issues. It is critical to ask yourself whether any of these are factors affecting your employee's performance.

In the next chapter, you'll learn how external motivations affect employee performance.

Notes

CHAPTER THREE

EXTERNAL MOTIVATION

Principle 3: *Individuals tend not to change their behavior unless they perceive the resulting consequences of such change to be more favorable than the consequences of their current behavior.*

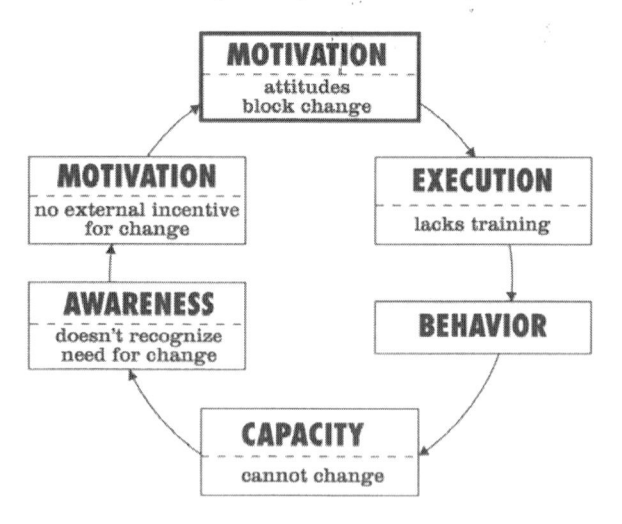

```
        MOTIVATION
        attitudes
       block change

MOTIVATION              EXECUTION
no external incentive   lacks training
    for change

 AWARENESS              BEHAVIOR
 doesn't recognize
  need for change

         CAPACITY
        cannot change
```

If insufficient external motivation is in place, a manager may need to alter or create new external incentives for change. An individual may not change an existing behavior or adopt a new behavior, because there is no apparent external motivation for such change. This involves individuals' unique, personal concepts of reward and punishment and how they individually perceive the consequences of their behavior. In other words, people do things they believe will result in attaining desirable consequences or rewards (in their terms) and avoid behaviors they believe will result in undesirable consequences or punishment. In this sense, actual or perceived consequences can control behavior.

BEHAVIORAL FLOW CHART

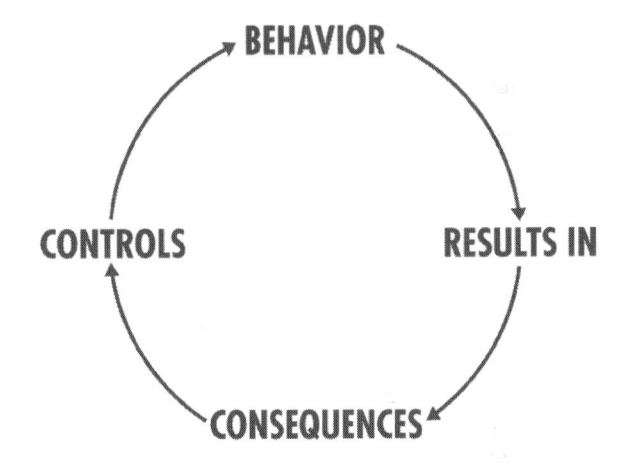

```
        BEHAVIOR
       ↗        ↘
  CONTROLS      RESULTS IN
       ↖        ↙
       CONSEQUENCES
```

Behavioral psychologists such as B.F. Skinner, often define a *reward* as "Any consequent event that tends to increase the probability of the behavior it follows."

Punishment is often defined as "Any consequent event that tends to decrease the probability of the behavior it follows." Utilizing this definition, a reward for one person may be a punishment for another. An individual who enjoys being in the limelight may get great pleasure from being called on to speak in front of a group, whereas a more reticent individual may find this extremely punishing.

The authors have observed a good example of this in Jim W.

> Jim was a production manager at a midwestern manufacturing plant. He had been at the plant for several years and not only had outstanding technical knowledge but was very adept and competent in dealing with people. When the vice president of operations offered Jim the position of plant manager, a significant promotion in responsibility and income, Jim declined. The vice president was surprised. Jim, however, perceived the additional responsibilities and necessary time commitment as a punishing consequence. He enjoyed the relative freedom of his current position, which he knew well, and he was not a particularly money—or status-motivated individual.

Jim's manager did not have a clear understanding of Jim's personal perception of reward and punishment.

It is also possible for you as a manager to inadvertently reward behavior you do not desire or discourage behavior that you do desire.

Fred B. clearly displays this behavior.

> Fred was the CFO at a large financial organization. His people continuously brought him reports and other documents that had errors he had to personally identify and fix. He was frustrated and angry that they were not doing their jobs.

"I'll Try" Is Not Good Enough ...

If you ask what was in it for them to continue this behavior rather than double-checking their work and correcting errors, the answer becomes obvious. There was nothing in it for them to catch the errors. Fred was only able to change the behavior when he changed the consequences for discovering errors and setting work back if there were errors. They knew that Fred would catch the errors, so they didn't need to (consciously or unconsciously). He was only able to correct the problem when he started sending incorrect work back (and back again, if necessary) until it was completed accurately.

The following example is an interesting parallel.

Studies of children who have been somewhat detached from their families have demonstrated that spankings may, in fact, be more rewarding than they are punishing. (The attention the child receives during the spanking may be more positive than the pain of the spanking is negative.) As a consequence, the parent may be reinforcing the undesirable behavior, not decreasing it. Conversely, when the child is behaving in a way the parent finds acceptable, the child is often ignored, decreasing the positive behavior.

In like fashion, many managers ignore good work and focus their attention only on employees' mistakes. Since attention of any kind is generally perceived to be more rewarding than lack of attention, the result may actually encourage further mistakes. Author Kenneth Blanchard clearly pointed out the importance of consistently rewarding good work in *The One Minute Manager*.

There are two basic forms of reward:

- the presentation of something the individual perceives as positive
- the withdrawal of something the individual perceives as negative

And there are two basic forms of punishment:

- the presentation of something the individual perceives as negative
- the withdrawal of something the individual perceives as positive

Time off from an unpleasant job may be rewarding. Conversely, overtime on a more pleasant job can be rewarding, as well.

In order for behavior to change positively, the consequence scale must tip in the appropriate direction. Any number of possible consequences may enter the mind of a person considering a requested behavior change. Since some of them may compete with others, the balance can be very delicate.

CONSEQUENCE SCALE

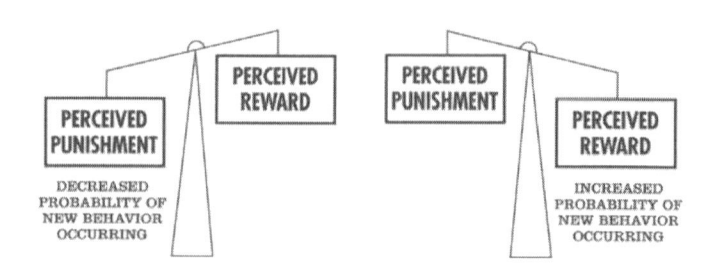

In several cases, competing consequences may occur. For example, an opportunity for advancement may be accompanied by the requirement to work long hours on a regular basis. While an individual may react positively to the perceived long-term rewards, the personal sacrifices that the additional time requires may tip the scale in a negative direction.

Another interesting example is delegation.

A manager may ask a subordinate to delegate and yet continue to reward the individual for results achieved through personal performance. The individual may want to delegate, but the time involved to do so might detract from short-term results and, in turn, diminish the manager's approval.

Positions requiring extensive travel may also force a choice between competing consequences. For some individuals, travel represents a positive consequence, and they readily accept such positions. For others, travel seriously disrupts their personal lives. They may reject such positions, even when they represent a significant promotion.

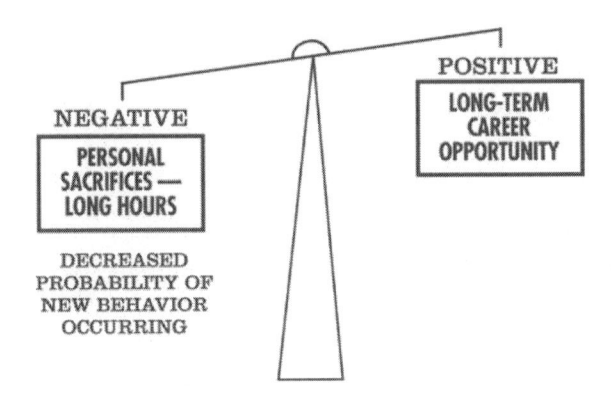

POSITIVE
LONG-TERM CAREER OPPORTUNITY

NEGATIVE
PERSONAL SACRIFICES — LONG HOURS

DECREASED PROBABILITY OF NEW BEHAVIOR OCCURRING

An excellent question to ask yourself when analyzing individuals' behavior and their likely reactions to the prospect of change is: "What's in it for them to continue doing what they are doing, and, in turn, what's in it for them to start doing what I want them to do?"

You must remember that a number of carefully balanced competing consequences may be influencing an individual's behavior at any given time. Although you may offer an individual what seems to you to be a desirable consequence for a behavior change, the perceived consequences of maintaining the existing behavior pattern may seem even more desirable to him or her.

You must assess the consequences carefully and see if you can change the balance scale in a way that will motivate the employee toward the behavior you desire.

Summary

External motivations can be defined through the concepts of reward and punishment. A manager should take into account an individual employee's own perception of reward and punishment before implementing consequences. What is a reward for one employee may be punishment for another.

In the next chapter, we'll move on to internal motivation and how it affects employee performance.

"I'll Try" Is Not Good Enough . . .

Notes

CHAPTER FOUR

INTERNAL MOTIVATION

Principle 4: *Individuals' self-perception, not reality, defines who they are and how they behave. Self-perception is resistant to change and can prevent individuals from altering their behavior.*

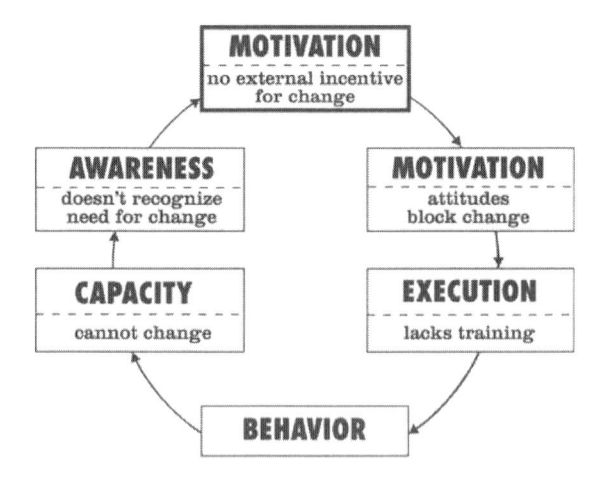

```
                    ┌─────────────────────┐
                    │    MOTIVATION       │
                    │ no external incentive│
                    │    for change       │
                    └─────────────────────┘
         ┌──────────────┐         ┌──────────────┐
         │  AWARENESS   │         │  MOTIVATION  │
         │ doesn't recognize│     │  attitudes   │
         │ need for change │      │ block change │
         └──────────────┘         └──────────────┘
         ┌──────────────┐         ┌──────────────┐
         │   CAPACITY   │         │  EXECUTION   │
         │ cannot change│         │ lacks training│
         └──────────────┘         └──────────────┘
                    ┌─────────────────────┐
                    │      BEHAVIOR       │
                    └─────────────────────┘
```

If a person's self-perception is fixed, it can produce conflicting internal motivation for making change. Individuals may have the capacity, awareness, and external incentive necessary to change, but the specific area of change may conflict with attitudes they hold regarding themselves. This can make change, at best, very difficult.

"I'll Try" Is Not Good Enough . . .

To explain briefly how and why this occurs, we'll use the analogy to compare the human thought process to the functioning of a computer system. Computers use two primary components of all data processing systems: hardware and software. The hardware consists of the silicon chips and assorted electronic equipment that are commonly known as the computer itself. There are powerful computers—such as an IBM supercomputer—that are capable of processing large volumes of complex information rapidly, and there are smaller, laptop varieties that, although extremely effective, have a lower capacity.

The hardware, however, is of absolutely no use unless it is fitted with software. The software instructs the computer how to handle and process information fed into it. The hardware and software together allow the computer to store and manipulate large volumes of information in the form of databases, and they allow one to refer to this information for evaluation, association, and decision making in relation to new information being inputted.

For the purposes of our analogy, we will refer to the brain as our "hardware." A few of us are fortunate enough to be an "IBM supercomputer," while the majority of us are more akin to the "laptop" variety. Our hardware defines our capacity and, as with computer hardware, requires software in order to work. Our "software" is built around our attitudes, values, self-images, and our various computing and filtering approaches that we acquire as we grow and learn.

Our behavior requires our hardware, but it operates through our software—our subconscious thought process. We all know people who have exceptionally good hardware but whose limited software results in not capitalizing on their capacity—for example, the genius mathematics whiz who is unable to get on the correct bus. Conversely, there are people with limited hardware whose advanced software enables them to more fully capitalize on their capacity and often overachieve.

As with a computer system, our human information processing system allows us to build a "database." It consists of all of the knowledge we have about the world we live in and the people and things that occupy it. Most importantly, however, our database includes all of the information we have acquired in relation to ourselves—who we are, our perceptions of what we are capable of becoming, and how we are supposed to act. This segment of our database defines the attitudes regarding ourselves and our self-images that we carry around in our minds.

The task of maintaining self-image is managed on a subconscious level. It works actively and predictably to ensure that we act in ways consistent with the reference points in our personal databases.

For example, individuals have ideas of how friendly they are. Their subconscious lets them know when they are too friendly or not friendly enough by making them feel uncomfortable and anxious. They do not have to think about how they should act—they just act! Their actions continually reinforce their attitudes and maintain consistency in their behavior. That segment of their software related to their self-images is the guidance mechanism for life and, once formulated, tends to be resistant to change. Consequently, attitudes incorporated in one's self-image can be a major barrier to behavioral change.

ATTITUDINAL REINFORCEMENT

```
        ATTITUDES/
        SELF-IMAGE

REINFORCES         GUIDES

          BEHAVIOR
```

One's behavior obviously does not remain exactly the same on a moment-to-moment, day-to-day basis, but it rarely moves outside a range called the "personal comfort zone." In discussing personal comfort zones, it is useful to think about the way thermostats control home furnaces. Set at sixty-eight degrees, your furnace most likely will come on when the temperature reaches sixty-six and will go off when the temperature reaches seventy degrees.

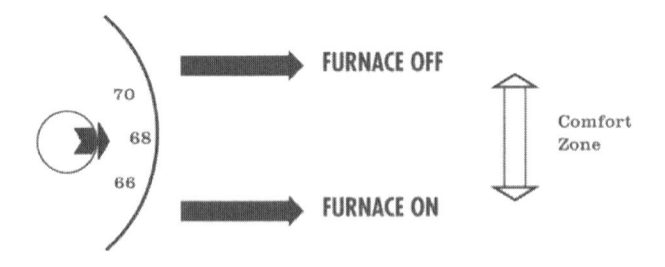

Individuals' software controls their personal comfort zones in much the same way. There is a range of behavior within which they can act and feel comfortable. If they get out of that range, they begin to feel anxious, tense, and "not themselves." Anxiety is a punishment, and relief from anxiety tends to be a reward. Consequently, they are punished for acting differently from how they perceive themselves to be and are rewarded by reduced anxiety by remaining in their comfort zone.

A good example of the effect of "the comfort zone" is Jim R.

> Jim was a thirty-two-year-old civil engineer who worked for a large engineering consulting firm. He was born and raised in a small town in Iowa. His father was a farmer, and while Jim was growing up, he spent most of his early years working on the farm. Jim was a good student, but because of his work at home, his involvement in the social aspects of school life was limited. He continued his formal education at the University of Iowa, where he excelled in the engineering program. As a junior engineer, Jim was outstanding. He had good technical skills and benefited from the strong work habits he developed as a youth. Highly regarded within the firm, he was given full consulting responsibilities after only three years.

Many aspects of Jim's job remained the same, but senior engineers were also required to participate actively in business development. This required calling on clients, making presentations, and developing new accounts. Jim wanted to achieve but felt terribly uncomfortable during sales calls. His voice would crack, and he found it hard to remember even the most basic engineering concepts. In customer-related activities, Jim was clearly out of his comfort zone. His anxiety level increased dramatically, and his motivation was to get back to where he felt he belonged—namely, the more technical aspects of his work. Jim told his supervisor that the selling activity was "just not for him." He soon began to find reasons to avoid getting out and making calls. He tended to lose himself in the technical details of his job. In sales, Jim attempted behavior that differed from how he perceived himself to be. His subconscious software was working hard to keep him behaving like himself. Jim had the capacity to do the job, but the struggle within him had a negative effect on his career. From such internal battles, which we all fight, comes the adage that you can be your own worst enemy.

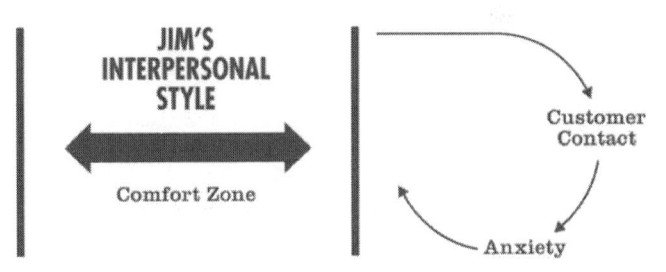

JIM'S INTERPERSONAL STYLE

Comfort Zone

Customer Contact

Anxiety

Some of the areas where personal comfort zones are readily revealed are as follows:

Personal
- Degree of dominance—how much are you really willing to listen versus feeling you have the answers and need to control the situation?
- Interactive style—are you collaborative, conciliatory, and one who readily capitulates?
- Involvement with the opposite sex—do you have a bias?

Work
- Career aspirations-what are your goals?, do you feel like you are heading towards them?
- Type of work-what type of work do you do? How is it defined?
- Achievement in one's work—do you feel like you are achieving what you want from your job, and are you being rewarded for your work?

One of the greatest impediments to employees' change may be the way they are mentally programmed. Their subconscious works hard to maintain the status quo. Change can be extremely difficult when individuals work against the way they perceive themselves to be. Some people, on the face of it, appear willing to change but struggle mightily and then backslide. It may take the use of strong external rewards and mentoring over time on the part of the manager to achieve change. Here you must ask yourself if you are dealing with an employee's attitude that runs counter to what you are trying to achieve.

Summary
A person's "hardware" (capacity) and "software" (attitudes and beliefs) often affect work performance. One's self-perception

"I'll Try" Is Not Good Enough . . .

can limit an employee's achievement, comfort level, and ability to change.

In the next chapter, we'll focus on education and training and see how they impact employee performance.

Notes

CHAPTER FIVE

LACK OF EDUCATION AND TRAINING

Principle 5: *Never assume that an individual has the necessary competence and training to do the job. You must probe and test for evidence and solicit feedback that the training exists.*

```
            EXECUTION
           lacks training

 MOTIVATION                    BEHAVIOR
  attitudes
 block change

 MOTIVATION                    CAPACITY
 no external incentive        cannot change
     for change

            AWARENESS
       doesn't recognize
         need for change
```

The Importance of Proper Assessment

In many respects, lack of execution skills may well be the easiest area in which to effect change in an individual's behavior. It may only require the application of appropriate training. Unfortunately, however, problems caused by a lack of training are frequently thought to be the result of motivational or other causes. As a result, they are dealt with in totally inappropriate ways. It may or may not be correct, for example, for a manager to think, *There is nothing wrong with George that working harder would not cure.*

Diagnosis of which of the problems are caused by a lack of training and which are not is a critical factor in the development process. It deserves more attention than it usually receives.

The Effect of Unwarranted Assumptions

Managers often make assumptions based on their own behavior. Because they have the knowledge and ability personally to perform competently in a particular position or to maintain a certain behavior, they may automatically assume that others also have that same knowledge and ability—or that they should be able to acquire it very quickly. This, however, is generally not the case. The discrepancy between the manger and the individual that they are working with can cause them both to become quite frustrated because of this false assumption.

Let's look at a specific example—John B.

> John was a thirty-six-year-old production supervisor. He was hardworking and performed well within the parameters and deadlines established by his manager. All of his performance reviews were excellent. Therefore, when his boss was promoted, John was the logical candidate to be the new production manager. When he took over the position, however, he began to have difficulty. Target dates were not met, and the flow

of work seemed to bog down. Plant efficiency and productivity decreased. It became apparent that John lacked competence in time management. He had not learned how to organize activities within a time frame either while he was growing up or in his business career to date. Previously, his manager helped structure his time, and he performed quite well. Therefore, it was assumed that John was fully prepared for the management role. Only when he was placed in the position was his lack of competence revealed.

Management assumed that John was competent in time management. Assumptions can cause problems for management and employees.

The Impact of Life Experiences and Conditioning

Each of us comes from a different learning background, and, consequently, our mix of competencies is obviously quite different. Clear examples of this phenomenon occur in the area of assertiveness. People who grow up in assertive families where parents encourage "on the table," direct communication can begin to develop an assertive competence early. Their growth years provide the opportunity to practice and refine it. For them, being assertive is a natural way of behaving, and there is a strong tendency for them to assume that it should be easy for others, as well.

For someone with a different background, however, one in which assertive behavior was discouraged or suppressed, the task becomes much more difficult. Asking such a person to exhibit assertive behavior is rather like asking a child who hasn't learned to read to recite from a book. Likewise, for nonassertive people, being assertive can seem equally awkward and inappropriate. Only over time, with practice and good coaching, can assertive skills become a more subconscious, natural activity.

We must also consider cultural differences. For example, Asian cultures generally tend to be far less direct in their communication than the majority of people found in the United States. Assertiveness may not come naturally. In fact, being too assertive may be viewed as showing a lack of respect, and it is inconsistent with their cultural norms. A website that outlines the various generalities about cultures and behaviors, www.GlobeSmart.com, can be very useful in this area.

In addition to life experiences, managers also need to be aware of a third impact on employee performance: training deficiencies.

Training Deficiencies

Training deficiencies can be defined as skills that employees lack and need to develop for minimum achievement on the job. Employees cannot train themselves; it is the responsibility of supervisors, managers, human resources staffers, and others to give employees necessary education.

Some areas where managers may observe training deficiencies include the following:

- assertiveness
- providing recognition
- persuasiveness

- time management
- planning
- organization
- social skills
- delegation
- participation of others in decision making
- technical skills

Managers must be willing to test individuals for personal skills and development needs through on-the-job assignments. This could take several forms, including

- transferring an individual to a new job assignment within the same department that requires learning a broader set of skills;
- assigning a special project to an individual within his or her current responsibilities that stretches the normal requirements of the position; and
- placing an individual on an ad hoc interdepartmental team that promotes peer-to-peer interaction and can help the individual gain a company-wide perspective.

Additional probing can be accomplished through "360-degree" performance assessments among peers, subordinates, and previous supervisors. This can help to garner a broader perspective for the individual. This feedback can be supplemented with an individual personal assessment administered by an independent company, if needed. There are many performance assessment tools available on the market for use by corporate managers. For more information on 360-degree feedback, visit http://en.wikipedia.org/wiki/360-degree_feedback.

Making undocumented assumptions about the competencies people have acquired and developed can be very misleading. Forcing people into situations for which they have not acquired the necessary skills can result in frustration, stress, and poor performance.

Remember that competencies must be taught, developed, and refined to a point of effectiveness over time.

Summary
Proper assessment, addressing unwarranted assumptions, allowing for life experiences, and training deficiencies can all affect an individual's performance. By utilizing testing methods and correcting training deficiencies, a manager can encourage stronger performance.

In the next section, we'll start learning about facilitating change and the methods to use for making change smoother for employees and management.

Notes

PART TWO

FACILITATING CHANGE

CHAPTER SIX

DEALING WITH CAPACITY ISSUES

Principle 6: *New behavior, called "overlays," can be learned by individuals without changing their genetic capacity or "hardwiring." These overlays allow individuals to behave or act in a different but more effective manner.*

Capacity Issues and "Learned Overlays"

Capacity issues cannot be altered, but at times, the way an individual behaves can be changed externally. A "learned overlay" is a behavior modification implemented through training and repetition. Learned overlays modify the way an individual acts in spite of his or her natural predispositions. It won't alter one's basic "hardwired" nature, but will instead create an overlay—a new, learned, external way of acting.

Some examples would include

- getting an introvert to display some extroverted behavior in spite of his or her genetic introversion;
- getting an individual who by nature has a short fuse and tends to "blow up" quite easily to display emotional control; and
- getting a "right-brain-dominant" individual to display some "left-brain behaviors," such as organizational skills.

Although overlays can be developed in some capacity areas, in the intellectual areas (analytical ability, abstract thinking, and creativity), the technique cannot be successfully applied. When it is attempted, the performance of the individual does not change, and people usually can see through the attempts to present a different behavior.

An overlay can be compared to an encapsulation. The natural tendencies are controlled and encapsulated, while the desired behavior is acted out on the surface. When achieved successfully, an outsider may not be aware that it is an overlay.

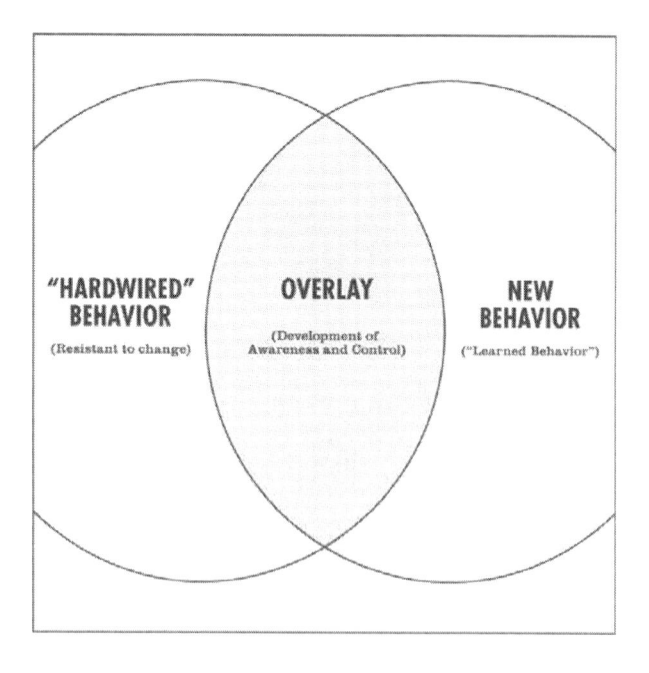

"HARDWIRED" BEHAVIOR
(Resistant to change)

OVERLAY
(Development of Awareness and Control)

NEW BEHAVIOR
("Learned Behavior")

A good example of a learned overlay was observed in Bill C.

"I'll Try" Is Not Good Enough ...

Bill was a successful software consultant. By nature, he was predisposed toward technical, analytical behavior. Bill, however, was genetically an introvert. His natural tendency was to retreat from people. (Extroverts are energized by people, whereas introverts are "drained" by people.) Bill's technical competence came naturally, but the people side was an issue. His position required that he interact both socially and on business matters with others. Because he was highly motivated to succeed, Bill learned to create an overlay. For example, Bill started keeping records of his clients' birthdays and sending cards on the appropriate dates. When he visited a client's office, he made it a point to talk to the receptionist and also take the time to ask his client how his family was doing. Although he was still introverted by nature, the overlay allowed him to act in an extroverted manner. It was acting, however, since his true nature had not changed.

Overlays are produced by creating what can be conceived as a capsule over oneself. The natural behavior remains in the capsule through various methods of self-control, whereas the desired behavior is intentionally displayed on the outside. Overlays effectively draw on innate strengths and diminish or hide innate weaknesses. In Bill's case, through a list of desired behaviors, self-prompting, and self-discipline, he learned to display the necessary extroverted behaviors. This does not mean, however, that it was still not draining for him. At off-site meetings, he was still the first one who wanted to retreat to his room after the daily activities were over (a common introverted behavior).

Another good example is Amed W.

> Amed W. was an electrical engineer employed by a large Southern corporation. His technical skills were solid, and as a result, he was promoted into a management position. By nature, however, Amed was emotionally volatile. He tended to quickly explode when things were not done to his standard. Obviously, this tended to alienate him from many of those who worked for him. He created an overlay that allowed him to encapsulate the emotion and, on the surface, act in an assertive yet nonhostile manner. He still had the same feelings but contained them because of the learned overlay. He behaved in a much more desirable, productive manner.

Creating overlays can be rather complicated at times, and it requires the manager's assistance in establishing the necessary learned encapsulation of the hardwired behavior. Also, there may be other deficiencies entwined with the individual's behavior. The individual may have awareness problems, self-image problems, and so on that he or she may need to deal with.

Some keys to establishing an effective overlay are

- an awareness that an overlay is necessary to achieve the desired results;
- a list of daily reminders regarding the new, desired behavior that must be created;
- establishing prompts that are visible and assist in the ongoing awareness of the necessary, external behaviors that must be displayed;
- a written track of daily behavior and recording "slips" when they occur; and

- the manager providing ongoing feedback and reinforcing the new external behavior that the individual is displaying outside the overlay.

This area can be difficult to master and, at times, may require the assistance of an outside consultant to help filter out all of the variables and to help establish the overlay.

Summary
A person's inherent capacity for behavior can't be changed, but actual behavior can be changed. Through overlays that essentially overwrite a person's predispositions—through repetition and coaching—a manager can help an employee show better behaviors in the workplace.

Once capacity issues are addressed, managers can move on to awareness issues. The next chapter on deficiencies in awareness will help you deal with employees who need input on their problem behaviors.

Notes
_____
_____
_____
_____
_____
_____
_____
_____
_____
_____
_____
_____

CHAPTER SEVEN

CORRECTING DEFICIENCIES IN AWARENESS: FEEDBACK DEFICIENCIES

Principle 7: *Individuals, in order to create awareness, need consistent, specific verbal and written feedback. This is necessary in order to overcome interpersonal, systems, and internal screens (self-perception). This feedback must come from their manager and others with whom the individuals work.*

People generally operate with feedback deficiencies that hamper their ability to change. Remember that feedback deficiencies stem from three primary areas. We have defined those as interpersonal, systems, and intrapersonal deficiencies.

Interpersonal Feedback Deficiencies

These deficiencies occur as a result of a lack of feedback from others. Without feedback as to how we are coming across or handling ourselves with others, it is impossible to change. Referring to the Johari Window model previously mentioned in chapter 2, you will recall that change is most likely to occur when there is a large arena.

JOHARI WINDOW

SOLICITING FEEDBACK

	I know	I don't know
They know	I. **ARENA**	III. **BLIND SPOT**
They don't know	II. **FACADE**	IV. **UNKNOWN**

SHARING INFORMATION

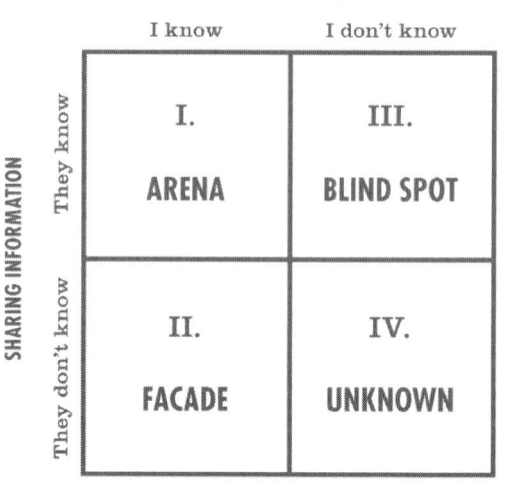

The Johari Window

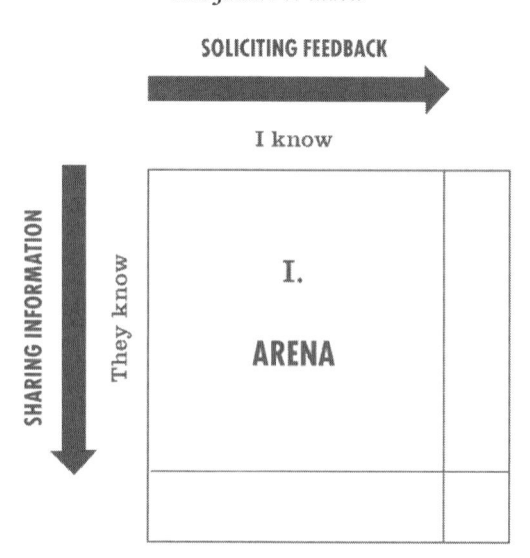

SOLICITING FEEDBACK →

SHARING INFORMATION ↓

I know / They know

I.
ARENA

"I'll Try" Is Not Good Enough . . .

Remember that, in a large arena, there is an ongoing and open flow of information between an individual and others. This open flow of information allows an individual to readily identify areas of interaction that are ineffective or substandard. Oftentimes, clear and specific feedback alone is all that is needed for behavior change to occur.

The Johari Window model applies as fully to entire organizations as it does to individuals. For an organization to sustain maximum growth and change, it must facilitate a large arena among all of its members.

Feedback that is not specific, clear, consistent, and frequent may have little impact on behavior change. For example, a manager may indicate to a subordinate that improvement in organizational ability is necessary. Without further detail, however, this statement may be too general and can lead to misinterpretation (e.g., the manager may be concerned about how the subordinate organizes and utilizes time, whereas the subordinate may think the statement refers to disorderliness in work habits). When communication tends to be incomplete and confusing, it can lead an individual to fill in the blanks with faulty assumptions.

For example, if an individual is abrasive and is unaware of it, the feedback must indicate specifically all of the verbal and nonverbal behaviors (eye contact, posture, etc.) that are interpreted as abrasive by others.

In order to ensure effective interpersonal feedback, it is important to

- back up oral feedback with specific, detailed, written communication—the use of e-mail can be a good way to do this;
- check clarity of feedback by requesting that the individuals involved specifically report back to you what they have been told;
- make contractual agreements with individuals to provide feedback on a regular, frequent basis;
- administer feedback-soliciting tools like a 360-degree survey—for further information, visit http://en.wikipedia.org/wiki/360-degree_feedback; and
- track such things as the "ask/tell ratio." *Ask* means asking good questions that cause people to think and grow in their problem-solving ability. *Telling*, on the other hand, tends to create a dependency on the manager for all of the answers and does not encourage people to further develop their problem-solving ability.

Based on our years of experience with employees, we've found that the most competent managers—those who are not only concerned with getting the job done but are equally concerned about developing their people—tend to have at least a fifty-fifty ask/tell ratio and preferably a seventy-thirty ask/tell ratio.

Systems Feedback Deficiencies

These deficiencies result whenever processes or systems we rely upon fail to provide us with the information we need to properly control them.

"I'll Try" Is Not Good Enough . . .

Brent W. is a clear example of this type of deficiency.

> Brent was president of a steel products manufacturing company. A graduate engineer, he worked in that field for several years before moving into management. His managerial experience before assuming the presidency was focused heavily on manufacturing. During his first year as president, the economy was strong, and the sales volume was high. He focused his efforts on building a quality product and developing a substantial inventory. During his second year as president, the economy began to retreat, and sales dropped precipitously. His business, which had been quite profitable, began to show substantial losses. He began to get a great deal of pressure from the parent company to control his losses and put the company back on sound financial footing. His balance sheet, however, continued to deteriorate, and at the end of the second year, he was terminated.

In reviewing this example, consider the following: What factors led to Brent's downfall and why? What could have been done to prevent it? Why was he unaware during his first year of the potential problems he was to experience during his second year?

You were correct if you concluded that Brent's downfall came primarily as a result of a systems feedback deficiency. In past positions, Brent had always worked within a small span of control where he could personally understand and monitor all activities going on around him. When he took over his new role as president, he continued behaving in much the same pattern as in the past. His span of control, however, was much too large, and his ability to comprehend and control events was soon exceeded. He did not recognize until it was too late the need to develop systems that could provide him with the necessary information on inventory, interest expense, and labor costs, among other things. During inflationary times, these areas were masked. As the recession took hold, however, he was forced to examine these areas in more depth and became painfully aware that his inventory, interest expense, and labor costs were considerably out of line. His balance sheet was a disaster. Had he been aware of the necessity for proper systems feedback procedures—or if company executives and the board had focused his attention on these areas—Brent's collapse might have been prevented.

Correcting Feedback Deficiencies

In order to correct feedback deficiencies, having clear standards of performance can help businesses track behavior. These standards are the road marks and milestones that can spell the difference between the success and failure of a business. They vary from business to business, but all businesses have them.

If it is determined, for example, that restaurant customers calling to make reservations hang up the phone after it rings four or five times, the standard of performance must be to answer all calls in three rings or less. Such standards can be elevated if they are determined to be too low—or lowered if determined to be too high. However, it is important that the standards be clearly stated and obvious to those who must maintain them.

Charting and journal keeping are useful ways of maintaining a high level of performance. When people count,

"I'll Try" Is Not Good Enough . . .

monitor, and record their own behavior, self-awareness and self-control increase.

Setting standards of performance and charting results are key elements in correcting systems feedback deficiencies.

In order for charting and journal keeping to be successful, it must start from the top with a strong commitment on the part of the president and CEO. In our experience in the workplace, we have observed that charting and journal keeping will taper off if it isn't encouraged and enforced.

Some of the items that can be counted and charted in order to correct feedback are as follows:

number of units produced per hour	makeup of clientele
number of sales calls made per hour	number of phone calls made
time required to respond to a request	inside sales per shift
number of accident-free hours	product mix
utilization of time	potential cost per item
inventory costs	revenue by time segment/product

Interestingly enough, when charting is discontinued, the level of new behavior attained tends to drop off, while the individual's perception is that it is holding steady. This only reinforces the concept that, without concrete data collection, individuals are not able to accurately judge their level of performance.

Intrapersonal Feedback Deficiencies

As previously discussed, people tend to selectively perceive information that is consistent with their belief systems and to screen out information that is inconsistent.

At the base of the brain is a network of cells that allows us to focus on certain aspects of a situation and to screen out other aspects. It makes us attentive to a particular conversation in a noisy restaurant and helps us shut out other conversations. As mentioned in chapter 2, individuals' screens are established by the *personal value or threat* of the information being received. Once individuals have established a mental "picture of reality," namely, "how things should be," the psychological screening device is responsible for maintaining the individuals' perceptions of reality. Information that is inconsistent with their belief systems are screened out, and information that is consistent (valuable to the individuals) is able to get through. The positive aspect is that it prevents them from information overload. The negative side is that they may miss important data that can help them be much more effective.

It is this screening device that explains why two people can go to a party and each experience a totally different event. One person believes that it is going to be a fun, enjoyable, and stimulating event, and, consequently, those facets of the party get through his or her screen. The other person believes it is going to be a boring, unpleasant, and uncomfortable event and, therefore, only sees the more negative facets of the event.

In order to make significant changes, individuals must learn to expand their belief systems. In order to do this, they must accept the basic tenet of "belief without data." In other words, they must accept the fact that there is a multitude of ways to look at situations and solve problems. For information to get through individuals' screens and allow them to develop new and creative approaches, they have to believe in the possibility of options other than their own.

For example, if one is looking for financing for a new home and believes that the only financing available is through banks, alternative methods of financing—even if they are plainly visible in newspapers, magazines, and so on,—tend not to get through his or her screens. An individual will inadvertently skim past them. In turn, this confirms his or her belief that there are no other alternatives available. When one is willing to entertain that alternative methods are possible, information needed to achieve the objective is much more likely to get through the screens and emerge into awareness.

In Bill L., you can see this screening process.

> Bill was an engineer in a large international manufacturing company. He could be very abrasive with people and had left some of the office staff in tears. Interestingly enough, because of his self-perception, he completely screened out people's reaction to him. He had been criticized in this area by his manager in the past, but it didn't get through. It was only when he was forced to meet with his boss and his peers and given concrete, clear examples that a breakthrough started.

Lack of awareness that is caused by intrapersonal feedback deficiencies is dealt with in much the same way as other awareness problems. To ensure that information gets through an individual's screens, it should be

- w*ritten*—written information is more difficult to reject than other forms of feedback and has greater surface validity;
- c*ollective*—collective information from more than one individual, especially when there is a strong sense of agreement, tends to have a much better chance of breaking through an individual's screen and being accepted as fact than information coming from a single source. We know, for example, that information reported objectively, such as 360-degree feedback, usually impacts an individual's attitude far more than one-on-one feedback; and
- f*requent*—feedback should occur frequently in order for an individual to assess whether or not he or she is making changes or falling back on old patterns.

In addition, the lack of ownership may be an important factor when dealing with intrapersonal awareness deficiencies. When individuals don't have a sense of ownership of their behavior, the information that they need to solve problems may not get through their screens. This was the case with Jan (see chapter 2), where she unwittingly maintained ownership that should have been passed on to those who worked for her. They didn't have to be responsible for solving the problems in the store, because, on a subconscious level, they knew that she would catch everything. The information to function effectively was being screened out.

Summary

Feedback deficiencies can have enormous effects on employee performance. Interpersonal feedback deficiencies are those that affect a person's relationships with others. Systems feedback deficiencies are those inherent in an organization's process or system that affect reporting and information. Intrapersonal feedback deficiencies are those within someone's personality that affect his or her perception of the world and the responses to it.

Feedback deficiencies can be corrected and modified to enhance employee performance.

In the next chapter, we'll review the concept of external motivation and its effect on performance.

Notes

CHAPTER EIGHT

CREATING EXTERNAL MOTIVATION

Principle 8: Individuals must have greater incentive to change their behaviors than to leave their behaviors unchanged.

The desire for change is a function of an individual's perception of the consequences of changing. As a manager trying to encourage change in a subordinate's behavior, you must offer a reward system for the desired new behavior that outweighs the reward system for the existing behavior. You must understand what consequences are attractive to the individual and how he or she relates to the behavior you desire.

Bob J. is a good example of this.

> Bob, manager of a retail building products company, had a work crew of fifteen in the yard, many of whom had been with the company for a long time. Bob was known among these employees as a detached and somewhat negative person. After attending a management seminar, however, he decided that he was going to be much more positive with people than he had been in the past. His office overlooked the yard, and when he saw the crew together, he made an effort to go out and positively interact with them. Concerned about disrupting their work, he did this

during break times when he would comment on their work, families, and so on. To Bob's surprise, the crew's work performance deteriorated. He concluded that they felt he was getting soft and, consequently, were loitering more and taking advantage of him.

Let's examine Bob's predicament utilizing the so-called SBC (situation, behavior, and resulting consequence) approach. While Bob learned a useful lesson during the management seminar, the approach he put into practice was ineffective. In order for Bob to realize the desired effect, his positive interaction with the crew needed to be a consequence of their working hard and effectively.

SITUATION (S)	BEHAVIOR (B)	CONSEQUENCE (C)
Work Environment ▶	Crew Not Working ▶	Bob Pays Attention ▶
Work Environment ▶	Crew Working ▶	Bob Ignores ▶

SITUATION (S)	BEHAVIOR (B)	CONSEQUENCE (C)
Work Environment ▶	Crew Not Working ▶	Bob Ignores ▶
Work Environment ▶	Crew Working ▶	Bob Pays Attention ▶

Overcoming external motivation deficiencies is essentially a matter of adjusting consequences.

Ask yourself what's in it for the individual to continue what he or she is doing versus the consequences of doing what you want him or her to do.

For SBC to be effective, try using the following concepts:

Focus on the positive. Eliminating a negative factor does not ensure the substitution of a positive factor. Ask yourself not what you are trying to eliminate, but what you are trying to substitute in its place, and then focus your efforts on rewarding that behavior.

> Marcia V., a vice president in a large retail company, was concerned about the abrasive, noncooperative behavior of a division general manager who reported to her. After fully analyzing the situation, she discovered that she was rewarding this behavior through her increased interaction with the supervisor when such behavior occurred. She decided to start ignoring it to see if it would decrease. In fact, the individual did become less abrasive but, much to Marcia's surprise, the person was not more cooperative. She had decreased *temperamental* behavior but had not taught and reinforced the supervisor the reciprocal *cooperative* behavior.

Reward improvement. Behavior is not learned in a one-time effort. Many of us make the mistake of assuming that telling somebody to change ensures that the change will occur. Behavior change comes only through systematic and frequent rewarding of the desired behavior. It is, therefore, as important to reward approximations of new behavioral goals as it is to reward fully successful efforts. In trying to develop cooperative behavior, for example, rewards must be given for early attempts toward cooperation. As better developed forms of the desired behavior emerge, they must be rewarded accordingly. It is a process of steps—crawling before walking, walking before running.

Recognize the existence of competing consequences. It is discouraging when we try to convince subordinates to change their behavior only to find that the rewards we offer seem not to encourage the change we desire. Managers confronted with this situation must analyze what rewards subordinates perceive for current behavior and to realize that behavior that has been consistently rewarded for a long period of time is highly resistant to change. The following statements summarize the dynamics involved in this process.

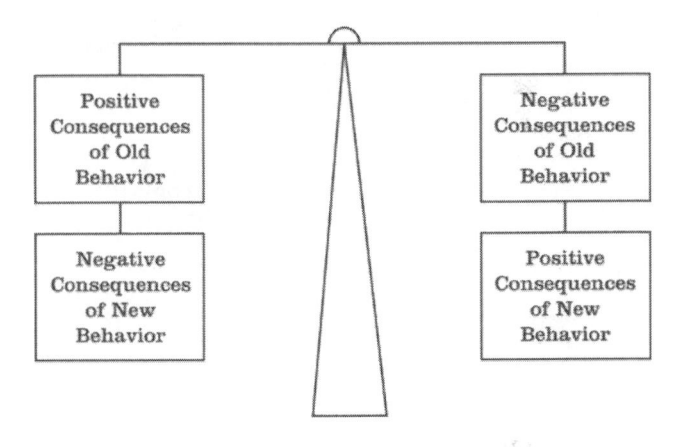

```
┌─────────────────┐                    ┌─────────────────┐
│    Positive     │                    │    Negative     │
│  Consequences   │                    │  Consequences   │
│     of Old      │                    │     of Old      │
│    Behavior     │                    │    Behavior     │
├─────────────────┤                    ├─────────────────┤
│    Negative     │                    │    Positive     │
│  Consequences   │                    │  Consequences   │
│     of New      │                    │     of New      │
│    Behavior     │                    │    Behavior     │
└─────────────────┘                    └─────────────────┘
```

Focus on nonmonetary rewards. Research has shown that monetary rewards may not be possible or essential in order to achieve sustained behavioral change. Therefore, you may well need to focus on nonmonetary rewards. Nonmonetary rewards that can be effective in this regard include the following:

- recognition from the manager
- status
- positions of more responsibility
- involvement in decision making

- achievement opportunities
- opportunities for creativity

Behavior changes slowly. Don't expect immediate and dramatic change. Old behaviors took a long time to develop; the shaping and conditioning of new behaviors also can take a long time. Many managers have poor systems for recording behavior change and often quit trying when subtle but important changes are actually occurring. A proper recording system notes even the most subtle behavior change. For example, an individual may increase his or her participation in meetings, but unless it is tracked and recorded, the difference may not be perceived.

Take care not to reward the behavior that you are trying to eliminate. The manager who interacts with subordinates only when they are in trouble and ignores them when they are performing adequately is only reinforcing and aggravating the situation.

As behavior begins to change, it needs to be rewarded intermittently. In our experience, we've found that once a behavior is established, rewarding it intermittently rather than continuously increases the strength of the new habit. This is the "slot machine" principle. Although the rewards are infrequent, the person expects them and in turn maintains a high level of performance. Be careful, however, not to discontinue the reinforcement, because this may cause regression to earlier behavior.

Summary

External motivations consist of rewards (monetary and nonmonetary) that reinforce an employee's improved performance. Utilizing situation, behavior, and consequence, intermittently rewarding behavior has the most positive effect.

"I'll Try" Is Not Good Enough . . .

In addition to external motivation, internal motivation also impacts employee performance. We'll discuss that in the next chapter.

Notes

Chapter Nine

Altering Internal Motivation

Principle 9: *Meaningful and lasting change may require that individuals alter the way they perceive themselves. It requires patience and discipline in order to achieve this. Self-perception can be altered, but not without real effort. It requires a well-thought-out plan, strong rewards, and discipline.*

Lasting behavior change may require a change in the software that controls an individual's self-perception. Self-perception, as previously mentioned, describes individuals' collections of beliefs and attitudes about themselves and what they can and cannot do. One's experience shapes self-perception, but it is not the actual events that become part of an individual's picture; it is his or her interpretation of those events. It is then reinforced by the way he or she engages in internal dialogue. The picture may or may not be consistent with reality.

INTERNAL MOTIVATION

ATTITUDES/SELF-IMAGE → BEHAVIOR → SELF-TALK → REINFORCES → (ATTITUDES/SELF-IMAGE)

Internal Dialogue

A person's self-perception affects his or her internal thoughts, and this internal dialogue can affect behavior. An inept manager may inadvertently reinforce a false negative or positive perception on the part of the individual. Negative internal dialogue reinforces and perpetuates negative behavior and can cause an individual's effectiveness to decline dramatically. Positive internal dialogue, on the other hand, can have the opposite effect.

Here are two examples of how Judy G. and Frank C. are showing how environment and internal dialogue interact to produce and reinforce an individual's self-perception.

> Judy G. was raised in a small, rural New England town. She had above-average intelligence but would be con-

sidered fairly average in most other ways. In her small town, however, she was able to excel both socially and academically. She received positive feedback from her environment, which resulted in positive internal dialogue. Judy began to develop a picture of herself as a confident, competent, socially skilled person. She continued to reinforce this attitude throughout her high school years by her positive internal dialogue, which was also prompted by the external feedback she received.

Frank C. was raised in a large, sophisticated, urban area on the West Coast. Although his intelligence and social competence were above average, he received little positive feedback from his environment regarding his personal effectiveness. Most people around him appeared to Frank as equally effective or more so. As a consequence, Frank's internal dialogue perpetuated an attitude of being average, both intellectually and socially. Throughout his formative years, his internal dialogue continued to reinforce this attitude, limiting his self-confidence.

This is an interesting situation. We have two people with roughly equivalent basic competencies and abilities. When both were transplanted into a working environment, how do you think they reacted? If you guessed that Judy was an achiever, you're right. Once again, people are drawn to act in keeping with the attitudes they hold about themselves. Internal software is the guidance mechanism, telling them where they belong and how they should function.

Judy continued to display confidence both in problem solving and as a supervisor. As a result, her achievement level was high, perpetuating positive feedback from the outside and continuing positive internal dialogue. This, in turn, reinforced her positive mental picture.

Frank's accomplishments were modest. He did not have a mental picture of himself as a particularly competent or confident individual. In his working environment, the information that got through his screens was consistent with his set of beliefs about himself. He did not strive to achieve, because his self-image led him to believe that he belonged in the middle group rather than among the leaders. As he acted on this attitude and received feedback consistent with it from his environment, it served to perpetuate his negative internal dialogue and the maintenance of his self-limiting attitude. If questioned about Judy, Frank would almost surely say that she had competence and talents exceeding his own.

To encourage a self-sustaining and high level of achievement in your subordinates, *you must help them develop attitudes consistent with the level of achievement necessary in their jobs and careers.* People must believe in what they can accomplish in order to accomplish it. Remember, individuals' subconscious self-perceptions work to maintain the status quo of their behavior. Trying to act differently throws them out of their comfort zone. They can find it very disconcerting to continue behaving that way.

In this situation, one of the keys to lasting change is to produce a change in attitudes. Individuals can struggle when they try to change behavior without first changing aspects of a limiting perception. It is not practical to push them to do something on a conscious level when they feel it is not "them" on a subconscious level. To do so may result in a temporary change of behavior, but it is one that will not be maintained. (This is the reason people with a self-perception of obesity go on diets and lose weight but find it very hard to keep it off. Their self-perception causes them to eat and regain the weight, and they end up "the way they belong.")

The same principle applies to people who have a self-perception of mediocrity in their achievement level. They feel uncomfortable if they push themselves to achieve too much and find it hard to sustain lasting performance improvement.

On the other hand, those fortunate enough to have developed an expansive self-image can be pulled by their positive attitudes toward success and achievement in all facets of their lives.

Your task in managing for change is to learn how to alter the attitudes of those who work for you when it is appropriate to do so. This involves a three-step process.

1. Help an individual identify and discontinue an internal dialogue that is maintaining self-limiting behavior.
2. Alternatively, performance-oriented internal dialogue must be substituted.
3. This new internal dialogue must be reinforced by frequent and consistent feedback from the manager.

Let's examine each of these steps in more detail.

Eliminating Negative Internal Dialogue

Before an individual can alter limiting internal dialogue, it must be identified. It can be done by looking for those areas in which the individual has to push the hardest in order to

"I'll Try" Is Not Good Enough . . .

sustain performance. This is generally an indication that the individual is working against a self-limiting attitude.

In order to help others, it can be very helpful to look at yourself. What are some self-limiting statements you make to yourself in terms of your current mental picture? How do they impact you? This can clearly help you in managing change in others.

1. At work

_____
_____
_____
_____
_____
_____
_____
_____
_____

2. Personally

_____
_____
_____
_____
_____
_____
_____
_____
_____
_____

3. Other

_____
_____
_____
_____
_____
_____
_____
_____
_____
_____
_____
_____

Self-Limiting Internal Dialogue

A survey sheet like this can be helpful for you to help an individual identify limiting internal dialogue. Once problem areas have been isolated and discussed, the self-limiting internal dialogue must be confronted strongly. The manager must help the individual evaluate his or her true potential in those areas. It is from this discussion that new, positive, alternate internal dialogue can be formulated.

Formulation of Alternate Internal Dialogue

Alternate internal dialogue items must be stated in the first person, present tense, and in a positive manner. For example, you might discover that an employee has a self-limiting attitude about organization, and the internal dialogue is, *I am basically a disorganized person who has a hard time getting things done on time.* The alternate internal dialogue statement might be, *I am an organized person who orders my activities in such a way that they get done in a timely manner.* It is important that the dialogue be affirmative and in the present tense—not "*I can*" or "*I will try.*" *Try* is the worst of all, because it gives the person an "out." It must be clear that this is not something one will *try* to do. It is something he or she *will* do.

When individuals talk to themselves, they talk in words, pictures, and feelings. They not only say the words, but they also see themselves in the situation. Individuals who engage in negative internal dialogue regarding organization, for example, tend to picture situations of disorganized behavior as they internally dialogue about it. Therefore, in order to develop new behavior, an individual must learn to picture alternate forms of behavior. The disorganized person needs to learn to envision him or herself behaving in an organized manner. Remember, behavior change tends to come slowly, and, as a consequence, an individual should—as a rule—not try to influence more than one self-limiting attitude at a time.

It is desirable to ask the individual to write down the alternate, positive, internal dialogue statements so that they can be reviewed daily. Following are some examples of negative internal dialogue and appropriate internal dialogue alternatives.

Negative Internal Dialogue
- I am a rather sloppy person whose affairs are always in a mess.
- I am a shy person who finds it hard to initiate contact with other people.
- I am a person who tends to keep my opinions to myself rather than sharing them openly one on one or in a group discussion.

- I find it difficult to make decisions unless I have all of the facts.
- I am a very volatile person who tends to be quick tempered.
- I prefer to work alone and find it hard to share responsibilities with others.

New Internal Dialogue

- I am an organized person who deals with my affairs in an orderly and systematic manner.
- I will initiate interaction with others in a self-confident, effective, and straightforward manner.
- I am a person who readily contributes during a meeting and stimulates discussion.
- I will act very decisively even if I don't have all of the facts when I realize that a decision is necessary.
- Even though I have strong feelings about issues, I will control my emotions and display them only when I choose to.
- I will share both responsibility and accountability with others and feel good about leveraging my efforts.

Outside Reinforcement

A change in attitude requires that the present self-limiting internal dialogue be *challenged* by the manager, not *accepted*. It must be reinforced from the outside in order for it to be most effectively maintained. Through ongoing discussion, managers gradually assist in changing their subordinates' pictures of who they are and what they can do.

Winning athletic coaches have utilized these principles for years. Too often, however, managers reinforce and perpetuate negative attitudes rather than building new and more positive ones. In other words, they focus on subordinates' weaknesses,

"I'll Try" Is Not Good Enough . . .

reinforcing their continued perception of themselves as ineffective. It is important to learn to talk to people in a way that encourages them to have positive internal dialogue. For example:

"You are basically organized; you just need to refine your skills in that area."
"You are basically assertive; you just need to express yourself more consistently."

Positive ongoing interaction and support of others, coupled with individuals' positive internal dialogue over time, can alter their attitudes and produce lasting behavior change.

Annette J. is a good example of this.

> Annette was an intelligent, twenty-nine-year-old customer service manager in the regional office of a large national manufacturing firm. When customers called in requesting assistance, she was at her best. She was friendly, knowledgeable, and effective in handling such situations. When her manager asked her to help call on new clients, however, she became very tense, anxious, and ineffective. Her manager felt that she was extremely talented and wanted her to take a more active selling role, whereas Annette was on the verge of quitting because of those demands.

Some questions about this case are as follows:

- How would you assess Annette's attitude? Where is her internal dialogue positive, and where might it be negative?

- What might her manager be doing to encourage her negative internal dialogue?
- What could her manager do to develop her behavior and, in turn, a more positive attitude?

If you concluded that Annette has a negative attitude in the area of selling, you are correct. Her internal dialogue was as follows: *I'm good at backing up salespeople, but I'm not a salesperson myself. I am not persuasive, and I am ineffective in a sales presentation.* This internal dialogue, of course, reinforced her self-image and perpetuated her ineptness. Her supervisor reinforced this view by pointing out, "You do well when you are serving accounts, but you seem to have a great deal of difficulty in handling new sales. You are much less effective in that area than you are with existing accounts." Rather than helping her alter her pattern of behavior, her manager's comments continued to reinforce it.

If her boss accepted the task of encouraging her to prepare for a more active selling role, her new internal dialogue might be: *I am good at backing up the sales force, and I am a skilled and competent salesperson myself. I am knowledgeable in my field of endeavor and one who effectively builds and maintains sales relationships with new accounts.*

Her manager's comments to her might be as follows: "You have the knowledge and skills to be quite effective in sales, and you are rapidly developing your skills in that area. I expect that your rate of success will increase rather quickly as you become more relaxed about this new effort."

Summary

In summary, managers have the responsibility to help subordinates change attitudes and self-perception in order for them to realize their potential. For this to occur successfully, managers must

- challenge strongly and not accept attitudes that are blocking behavioral change; monitor them so they do not slip back and focus on the negative qualities they are trying to change;
- help subordinates visualize themselves in new ways through ongoing, one-on-one meetings focusing on positive internal dialogue;
- and watch for new, positive behaviors in subordinates and actively reinforce these behaviors when they occur.

Once internal motivation is in place, managers can prompt even stronger results with a positive climate for workplace change. The next chapter shows you how creating this atmosphere will benefit your employees.

Notes

CHAPTER TEN

CREATING A CLIMATE FOR DEVELOPMENT

Principle 10: *A developmental climate and proper training must occur for individuals to acquire the competence and skill sets to perform successfully in their positions.*

One reason people don't change is due to their lack of basic training. One of the errors a manager can make is to assume without documented evidence that an individual has the basic skills necessary to act assertively, to organize, to plan, to delegate, or to hold people accountable. Another common error is to assume that individuals alone can reach levels of development that enable them to behave effectively in all areas. It is critical to understand that insight alone may not produce the desired results. A development climate and plan must be created by the individual and the manager. This is necessary in order for subordinates to recognize their deficiencies and have the desire to pursue the necessary training to correct them.

In order to help develop your employees awareness, using the Managerial Grid can facilitate discussion of the effects of autocratic (produce or perish), laissez-faire (country club), indifferent (impoverished), middle of the road and a participative (team) approach.

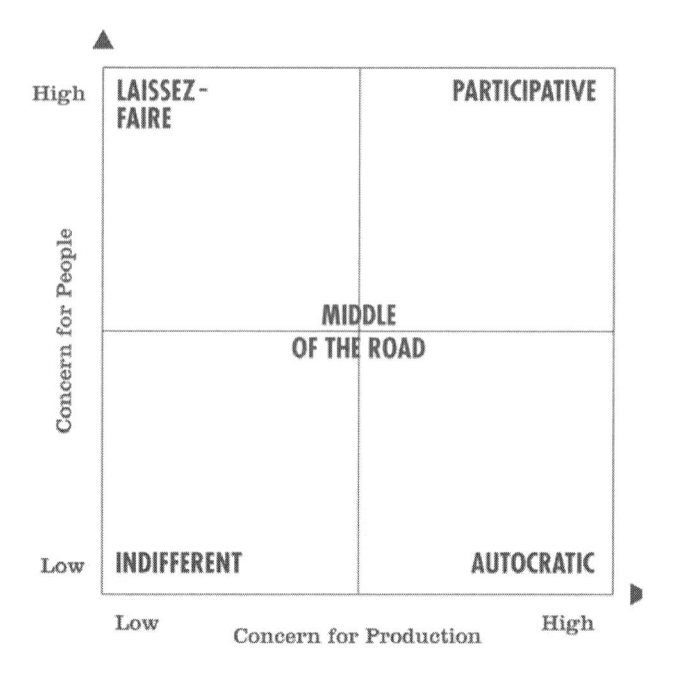

```
                 ▲
High  │ LAISSEZ-       │ PARTICIPATIVE
      │ FAIRE          │
      │                │
      │                │
      │          MIDDLE│
      │         OF THE ROAD
      │                │
      │                │
Low   │ INDIFFERENT    │ AUTOCRATIC     ▶
      Low    Concern for Production    High
```

Figure X. The Managerial Grid

Management style is a critical factor in the creation of a development climate. As shown in the grid, managers function along two dimensions (concern for production versus concern for people).

In the upper-left quadrant is the "laissez-faire" (country club) manager. Such managers are attentive to people, while their concern for production is secondary. In the lower left-hand quadrant is the "indifferent" (security-oriented) manager. These managers are neither attentive to people nor to production. In the lower right-hand quadrant is the "autocratic" (produce or perish) manager. Managers like these are very attentive to production, while attentiveness to people is of little concern. In the upper right-hand quadrant is the "participative" (team-oriented) manager, who is the true leader. Managers such as this are attentive to both production and people. Managers who try to be attentive to both people and production, but tend to vacillate in the process and have difficulty carrying it out, are called "middle-of-the-road" managers.

Managers fitting all five descriptions have been studied in depth by the authors. The research concluded that the highest-achieving managers fall in the "participative" category. Moderate-achieving managers fall into the "autocratic" category. The lowest-achieving managers are in the "indifferent" category.

An even more interesting finding is that subordinates appear to fall into much the same category as their superiors. The point is that the model one sets will be perpetuated throughout your organization.

Autocratic managers don't teach—they tell. Subordinates are not allowed to think for themselves, solve problems, or grow. They just carry out orders. This type of manager finds people only as a means to an end. There is little participation or collaboration. Schedules, rules, and punishment are used to achieve goals. In an attempt to alter autocratic behavior, it is helpful for the manager to track their ask/tell ratio. This is a journal that collects the number of times, when presented with an issue, the manager asks the subordinate to solve the problem versus telling the subordinate how to solve the problem.

Laissez-faire (country club) managers do not encourage a development climate. Rather, it tends to be without structure, and it promotes ambiguity rather than standards for personal growth. A focus on productivity is missing.

Indifferent (security-oriented) managers tend to evade and elude in order to keep their employment. Their primary concern is to maintain their positions and job security by not making mistakes.

Middle-of-the-road managers try to balance people needs and production but find it difficult and tend to compromise more than they should. Their focus is on maintaining the status quo.

Participative managers (high task, high people) are clearly what an individual should strive for. A large arena creates the best development climate. It not only promotes high standards of performance but also generates a positive, participative environment that allows subordinates to think for themselves and to grow through involvement in decision making and problem solving. Their ask/tell ratio tends to be quite high on the ask side. Sharing information tends to perpetuate the receiving of information from others.

As a side note, introverts have been found to be better listeners, whereas extroverts have a greater tendency to tell subordinates what to do. As a consequence, developing an ask/tell ratio that is high on the ask side may be somewhat more difficult for extroverts to master. For more information on introversion and extroversion, a book entitled *The Introvert Advantage: How to Thrive in an Extrovert World* by Marti Olsen Laney can be quite helpful.

Along with a managerial style understood and properly implemented, skills training programs are extremely important in preparing individuals to organize, manage time, make decisions, and so on. But without outside support and reinforcement in a proper development climate, these efforts can amount to little more than academic exercises.

In addition to training programs, apprenticeships and mentoring programs are also a powerful method for helping people to acquire competence. Individuals learn a great deal through modeling and imitation. Working closely with someone who has a high level of competence can dramatically facilitate behavior change.

Summary

By understanding your own placement on the Managerial Grid, your self-knowledge can help you learn to motivate, manage, and develop positive change in the workplace. Whether you fall into the category of autocrat, laissez-faire, indifferent, middle-of-the-road, or participative manager, managing your own attitudes and behaviors will have a positive effect on employees.

Notes
_____
_____
_____
_____
_____
_____
_____
_____
_____
_____
_____

CONCLUSION

Modifying people's behavior can be quite difficult and time consuming. In those individuals where there are major discrepancies in several areas, assessment and change techniques should probably not be attempted. The time on a manager's part that would be necessary would most likely outweigh the potential results. As you well know, a manager's time is limited and quite valuable. It should be deployed where the greatest impact can result.

We recommend that all managers go through a personal time analysis, looking at how they currently spend their time and what percentage of that time is spent working on the development of their people. This can be helpful in assessing and allocating development time and also in setting your overall priorities. Planning your time and deploying it where it counts the most is a key priority both in getting results and preparing the next generation for the management of the company.

With some people who have discrepancies, numerous factors may contribute to the discrepancies that exist between desired and actual behavior. In other situations, only one factor may account for the discrepancy needs to be addressed.

Creating behavior change can be a challenge, and it requires careful assessment of the individual. Even though an individual may have strong assets in some areas, working on his or her development needs can pay off. The change effort can be difficult, but it is definitely worth your time!

Managers must start with disciplined selection and hiring practices; they should then place employees into the right positions before beginning their development. Especially with new hires, managers must identify the gaps and quickly begin to deal with them before they get set in patterns that are not conducive to their success in the organization. As a result of companies' leadership and unique histories, they generally have unique cultures that develop over time. For newcomers, the "fit" can prove to be a big challenge. "Fit" must first be recognized so then it can be worked on from the beginning. This can assure a much smoother transition for the individual into the company. Often, however, the more experienced a new person is, the more difficult the fit may be.

Apart from what is genetically inherited, personalities and behavioral patterns start developing at an early stage of an individual's life. They are not easy to change. Given that truism, it is imperative that managers find ways to modify the organizational culture in order to encourage the development and adaptation of their employees' performance to the demands of their business and the marketplace.

It takes a conscientious effort on the part of management (who may already feel overextended) to devote the necessary time to meaningfully educate, coach, and mentor those who work for them. It is important that managers remind themselves to set aside this time in their schedules. One's role as a teacher and developer of people is critical for the future of the company.

Remember, behavior change comes slowly and takes a real effort. In the end, managers can grow exponentially by surrounding themselves with the best-developed talent. It is the mark of a successful manager and leader.

As you proceed down this journey, please feel free to call or e-mail us with your questions. We are more than willing to help.

Good luck.

> The Woodward Consulting Group
> (626) 272-8730

APPENDIX

Summary Checklist

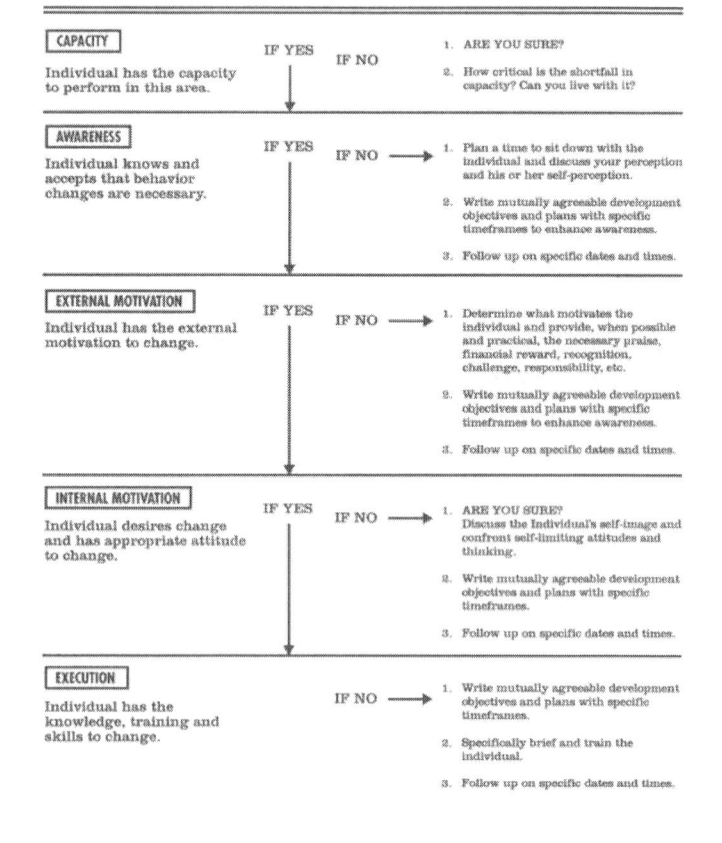

	IF YES	IF NO	
CAPACITY Individual has the capacity to perform in this area.	↓	→	1. ARE YOU SURE? 2. How critical is the shortfall in capacity? Can you live with it?
AWARENESS Individual knows and accepts that behavior changes are necessary.	↓	→	1. Plan a time to sit down with the individual and discuss your perception and his or her self-perception. 2. Write mutually agreeable development objectives and plans with specific timeframes to enhance awareness. 3. Follow up on specific dates and times.
EXTERNAL MOTIVATION Individual has the external motivation to change.	↓	→	1. Determine what motivates the individual and provide, when possible and practical, the necessary praise, financial reward, recognition, challenge, responsibility, etc. 2. Write mutually agreeable development objectives and plans with specific timeframes to enhance awareness. 3. Follow up on specific dates and times.
INTERNAL MOTIVATION Individual desires change and has appropriate attitude to change.	↓	→	1. ARE YOU SURE? Discuss the Individual's self-image and confront self-limiting attitudes and thinking. 2. Write mutually agreeable development objectives and plans with specific timeframes. 3. Follow up on specific dates and times.
EXECUTION Individual has the knowledge, training and skills to change.		→ IF NO	1. Write mutually agreeable development objectives and plans with specific timeframes. 2. Specifically brief and train the individual. 3. Follow up on specific dates and times.

ADVICE ON UTILIZING CONSULTANTS

If you decide to use a consultant for an outside perspective on your business, here is some advice to help you decide how, why, and which consulting firms can benefit you.

Consultants can be very effective in assisting you with helping your people make change, especially those that appear to be the most resistant to change. It is important to remember, however, that you—as the manager—have the primary responsibility for the growth and development of those who work for you. This is not something you can delegate to others—not to human resources departments or outsiders. Many of the next generation of management and leadership must come from those who work for you. For the company's long-term success, they need to be prepared. This preparation cannot happen in the last few months of a transition; it must occur over a rather lengthy period of time. Many managers think that their only function is to direct people and achieve the desired results for the company. This is obviously very important, but it is only part of their job. They must also think of themselves as teachers and mentors of the next generation. Assuring that people are prepared to step up when you are gone is a major function of your job as a manager.

Consultants are there to *assist* you in that job, not to do it for you.

There are a large number of consultants out there. It is important that when you engage one, you find the best possible individual available. Below are some things to consider before contracting with a consultant.

- Make sure that he or she has the necessary qualifications to perform to your expectations.
- There are a lot of consultants who have become consultants because they have either lost their previous positions or are in between positions. Many are still looking for a "real job."
- A good consultant must have the credentials and background to achieve the goals that you want accomplished and to meet your expectations.

In consulting, there is a lot of salesmanship, but there may be little substance. One can judge a good consultant not by his or her promotional materials but by the significance of his or her consulting experience and/or years of successful experience as a manager and consultant.

Do a thorough check of his or her background and experience. Has he or she served in meaningful, relevant positions? Probe for hands-on experience from the consultant where he or she had to deal with similar issues and problems that you face. If you work in a family business, experience in a family business is critical on the part of the consultant.

Look for lasting experience with clients. Many consultants work on short-term issues and are not invited back. Good consultants build a track record with their clients. Over the years, they maintain the respect of the client as a result of their visible competence and ability to get results.

Make sure that the fees are realistic for the assignment. Many consultants may charge far more than they contribute. This may be a result of the consulting firm's inherent fee structure and its reputation as a firm. It may also be the lack of knowledge regarding reasonable fees on the part of the management.

BIBLIOGRAPHY

Blanchard, Kenneth, and Spencer Johnson. *The One Minute Manager*. New York, New York: Berkley Publishing Group, 1982.

Blake, Robert, and Jane Mouton. *The Managerial Grid: The Key to Leadership Types*. Houston, Texas: Houston Gulf Publishing Company, 1964.

Bry, Adelaide. *Directing the Movies of Your Mind*. New York, New York: Harper and Row, 1978.

Collins, Jim. *Good to Great*. New York, New York: Harper Collins Publishing, 2001.

Herrnstein, Richard J., and Charles Murray. *The Bell Curve*. New York, New York: Free Press, 1994.

Holland, James G., and B. F. Skinner. *The Analysis of Behavior*. New York: McGraw Hill, 1961.

Keirsey, David, and Marilyn Bates. *Please Understand Me: Character and Temperament*. Del Mar, California: Prometheus Nemesis Book Company, 1984.

Laken, Allen. *How to Get Control of Your Time and Life*. New York, New York: Signet, 1974.

Laney, Mart. *The Introvert Advantage: Making the Most of Your Hidden Strengths*. New York, New York: Workman Publishing, 2002.

Luft, Joseph. *Group Processes: An Introduction to Group Dynamics*. Palo Alto, California: Mayfield Publishing, 1963.

Maltz, Maxwell. *Psycho-Cybernetics*. Englewood Cliffs, New Jersey: Prentice-Hall, 1960.

Schiffer, Fredric. *Of Two Minds: The Revolutionary Science of Dual-Brain Psychology*. New York, New York: the Free Press, 1998.

For more on this topic; right brain left brain quiz can be seen at http://www.intelliscript.net/test_area/questionnaire/questionnaire.cgi on "360-degree" feedback, visit http://en.wikipedia.org/wiki/360-degree_feedback

ABOUT THE AUTHORS

Philip B. Nelson, PhD

Philip Nelson was engaged as a management consultant in major corporations, fast-growth companies, and entrepreneurial ventures since 1974.

His consulting expertise included executive coaching and development, acquisition and mergers, organizational design and structure, program implementation, cultural assessment and change, executive selection, succession planning, family business transition, and board formation and development.

His clients included Fox Broadcasting Company, Foster Farms, Inc., J. P. Morgan, Millipore, Mattel, Inc., National Semiconductor, Hewlett-Packard, Clorox, General Electric, Pfizer Pharmaceuticals, American Broadcasting Company, Unisys, York International Corporation, the Urban Land Institute, the Wine Group, First Health, and Kysor/Warren.

His publications include The Integrated Management Development System, IEP, 1992, The Position Suitability Profile System, IEP, 1993, In Search of Mediocrity, Woodside Press, 1986, The Stress Analysis System, IEP, 1993, Recognizing and Redirecting Stress (video and workbook), Knowledge Resources, 1988, The Management Effectiveness

Survey, Interdatum, 1986 and Seven Secrets of Exceptional Leadership, Executive Books, 1997.

Before forming IEP Consulting, he was a senior vice president and co-owner of Interdatum, Inc., an international employment database company, where he ran their corporate publishing and consulting group.

Philip taught at the university level and served as a managing director of a day hospital/outpatient clinic complex. He was cofounder and codirector of the Vail Colorado Institute, a CME program where the focus was on current research and education in the areas of stress, human illness, change, and productivity.

Dr. Nelson has served on the boards of Foster Farms, Pepco, Stag's Leap Wine Cellars, and Syntrio.

Michael Paxton

Michael Paxton has a successful and extensive leadership background. His experiences include president of Pillsbury's baked goods division, CEO of Häagen-Dazs, CEO of Sunbeam's health and safety division, chairman and CEO of O-Cedar Holdings, Inc., and he is currently chairman of Transport America, a for-hire truckload carrier. He had the opportunity to lead both private and public companies.

Mike also had over twenty years of experience on public and private boards, including companies competing in the areas of medical devices, consumer package goods, pharmaceuticals, transportation, and communications. He is currently on the boards of Foster Farms, Inc., Transport America, Azteca

Foods, Inc., Gemini, Inc., and XATA Corporation (Nasdaq: XATA).

His excellent strategic skills have always been balanced with an understanding of the importance of day-to-day, hands-on attention to the business. Throughout his career, he has strived to build the best organizations and empower his employees to perform beyond their expectations.

Kirk Nelson, MFA

Teaching and mentoring have been a significant aspect of Kirk's career. Kirk taught at Loyola Marymount University from 2001-2006 and was a teaching assistant at the School of the Art Institute of Chicago in 2000. Currently, Kirk is a creative consultant/mentor and the website administrator for the Woodward Consulting Group. He was a principle in graphic design at Schlosberg & Co on the Eli Broad Celebration book and worked as a graphic designer for Phaedrus Productions.

Kirk continues to work in independent film production. He was the writer and director of the feature film *Humanoid* produced by David Schwimmer and Dark Harbor Stories, Inc. He is currently working as an independent film writer, producer, and director.

As a fine artist, Kirk had a solo show at Kim Light Gallery entitled "Fade to Black." He has also shown with Perpetual Art Machine in Miami, Scope Art Fair in London, LA ART in New York, and the Hayworth Gallery in Los Angeles. Kirk Nelson earned his undergraduate degree from Loyola Marymount University and his master's degree from the School of the Art Institute of Chicago.

Made in the USA
San Bernardino, CA
22 February 2014